Mutants, Clones, and Killer Corn

Mutants, Clones, and Killer Corn

Unlocking the Secrets of Biotechnology

Samantha Seiple and Todd Seiple

Lerner Publications Company ■ Minneapolis

For our parents—Anne, Sam, Freda, and Terry

Special thanks to the San Diego Public Library

Lerner Publications Company
A Division of Lerner Publishing Group
241 First Avenue North
Minneapolis, Minnesota 55401 U.S.A.

Website address: www.lernerbooks.com

LIBRARY OF CONGRESS CATALOGING-IN-PUBLICATION DATA

Seiple, Samantha.
    Mutants, clones, and killer corn : unlocking the secrets of
biotechnology / by Samantha Seiple and Todd Seiple.
        p. cm. — (Discovery!)
    Includes bibliographical references and index.
    ISBN 0–8225–4860–7 (lib. bdg. : alk. paper)
    1. Biotechnology—Juvenile literature. I. Seiple, Todd. II. Title.
III. Discovery! (Minneapolis, Minn.)
    TP248.218.S45 2005
    660.6—dc22   2004028049

Manufactured in the United States of America
1 2 3 4 5 6 – DP – 10 09 08 07 06 05

CONTENTS

INTRODUCTION

What do you get when you combine a firefly and a plant? A plant that glows in the dark. And what do you get when you combine a jellyfish and a mouse? A mouse whose whiskers, eyes, ears, skin, and organs turn fluorescent green under ultraviolet light.

These experiments weren't conducted in Dr. Frankenstein's laboratory. They go far beyond stitching together parts of different organisms. Instead, they involve transferring genes—the basic units of heredity—from one organism to another to create transgenic organisms. Scientists hope that these new plants and animals will help humans live better lives.

But why make glowing plants and animals? It can be difficult to tell if a gene transfer has been successful. But it is easy for researchers to find out if a jellyfish gene transplant has worked. All they have to do is pass a fluorescent light over the transgenic organism. If the organism glows, the gene is working.

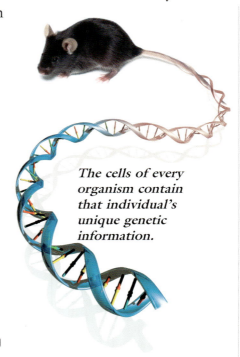

The cells of every organism contain that individual's unique genetic information.

In one highly publicized experiment, scientists inserted the gene that makes a jellyfish glow green into the eggs of rhesus monkeys. The researchers genetically altered 224 monkey eggs in this manner and then fertilized them. Of those 224 fertilized eggs, 40 began to grow and were implanted into 20 female monkeys. Five of the surrogate monkeys became pregnant. Three baby monkeys were born alive, but only one survived. The hair and fingernails of the two baby monkeys that had died glowed green under fluorescent light. The surviving baby monkey, whom researchers named ANDi, has the jellyfish gene in every cell of his body, but he doesn't glow—at least, not yet. The scientists are hopeful that ANDi may begin to glow as he ages. "We're at an extraordinary moment in the history of humans," said Gerald Schatten, a scientist on the research project.

ANDi is the world's first transgenic primate. (The group of animals called primates includes monkeys, apes, and humans.) This experiment could lead to a means of understanding primate development and diseases. For example, scientists studying cancer might be able to use the jellyfish gene to mark cancer cells. Then they would be able to use the green glow to monitor the spread of the disease.

Controversy goes hand in hand with genetic research. Although the scientific community considered the glowing-monkey research to be groundbreaking, critics thought it was abominable. "We condemn them for their philosophy that animals are nothing more than test tubes," said Peter Wood, a research associate with People for the Ethical Treatment of Animals (PETA). "And we believe this is another pipe dream of Frankenstein science."

Despite criticism of their research, scientists around the world are working on biotechnology projects. In the future, they expect to create more human-made plants and animals that go beyond Frankenstein.

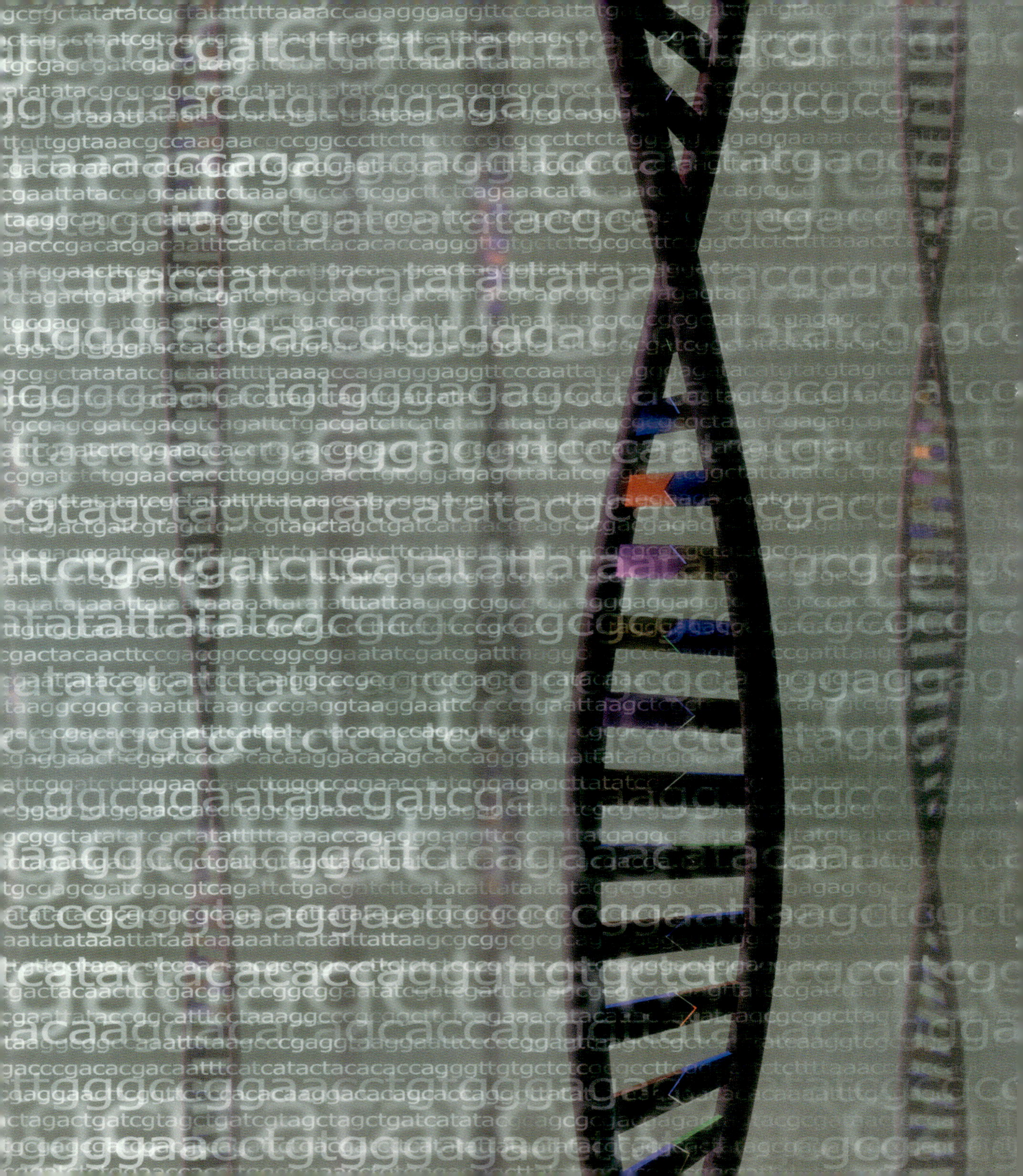

BIOTECHNOLOGY

'Tis strange—but true; for truth is always strange,
stranger than fiction. —Lord Byron, English poet

Truth is stranger than fiction in the field of biotechnology, where things that once were the workings of great science fiction books are quickly becoming part of our everyday lives. Although most people don't realize it, products of biotechnology touch our lives on a daily basis—from the cereal we eat and the soda we drink to the jeans we wear.

The word *biotechnology* refers to the use of living organisms or the cellular components of living organisms to create products for human use. The root word *bio* means "life," and the word *technology* refers to using scientific methods to solve problems and to create useful products. Biotechnology encompasses a variety of sciences and technologies. It includes cloning, genetic engineering, tissue engineering, and related techniques.

Hungarian engineer Karl Ereky first used the term in 1919, but people have been using biotechnology techniques since prehistoric times. Humans first applied biotechnology to improve their lives around 8000 B.C., with the domestication of livestock and crops. Over the course of a few thousand years, humans discovered that selectively breeding livestock and crops with the most desirable characteristics produced a superior food supply.

Opposite: *DNA (deoxyribonucleic acid) is the molecule that contains genetic information. It has become a symbol of biotechnology.*

Breeding and Hybridization

For centuries farmers have practiced selective breeding—breeding plants and animals for specific desirable traits. To grow large ears of corn, farmers planted seeds that came from large ears of corn. This process was repeated each planting season. Over time, the yield of large ears increased.

Individual organisms usually breed only with others of the same species. For example, a leopard can't mate with a wolf and produce a spotted cat-dog. The genetic boundaries between unrelated species can't be crossed due to a number of differences called isolating mechanisms. Physical barriers may separate the species. Differences in mating rituals from species to species may prevent breeding. Some species are fertile only at one specific time of the year that may not coincide with another species' period of fertility. And usually sperm from one species is chemically incapable of fertilizing an egg from another species.

But occasionally crossbreeding—the mating of individuals of different, closely related species—takes place. For example, horses and donkeys are different species, yet they can mate and produce hybrid (mixed) offspring. Hybrids are almost always sterile—the offspring are unable to reproduce. A mule is the sterile hybrid offspring of a female horse and a male donkey. Hybrids rarely occur in nature.

Farmers work the fields in this Egyptian painting from the thirteenth century B.C. Ancient Egyptians practiced selective breeding of animals and plants to improve livestock and crops.

During the same time period, living yeast cells were being used to ferment beer and wine and to produce bread and cheese. It took thousands of years, however, before humans understood how and why these processes worked.

MODERN BIOTECHNOLOGY

After scientists gained a thorough understanding of cell biology and genetics, they began to experiment with the idea of creating specialized living organisms that would help humans in their daily lives. The goals of scientists included increasing food production, decreasing environmental pollution, producing medicines more cheaply to make them accessible to the poor, and growing human body parts for transplants. This was just the beginning of a new age of controversial experiments.

In 1982 the first genetically engineered product was made available for human use. The product was insulin. Insulin is a hormone that brings sugar from the blood into the body's cells, where it provides energy. Some people who have the disease called diabetes need daily injections of insulin to keep their bodies working properly. Doctors originally got insulin for their patients from pigs and cows. Then scientists figured out how to use biotechnology to make large supplies of insulin. They genetically modified a common bacterium, *Escherichia coli* (or *E. coli*), to make it produce the hormone.

In 1994 the first genetically engineered food product for human consumption became available in the United States. It was a tomato named the Flavr Savr. It had been genetically modified so it wouldn't rot as quickly as unmodified tomatoes. There was little protest from the public regarding the consumption of genetically modified (GM) foods. In fact, the demand for Flavr Savr tomatoes was so high that it was difficult to keep stores stocked with them. After a few years, however, the tomatoes were taken off the market, largely because they were too costly to produce. They also were more delicate than unmodified tomatoes, so they became damaged more easily during shipping and handling.

Despite the initial popularity of the Flavr Savr tomato, it wasn't long before activists in the United States and abroad began protesting against the genetic modification of food and animals. The controversy has been building. Activists question the safety of GM products and the ethics of genetically altering plants and animals.

When Science Experiments Go Wrong

In the 1950s, beekeepers in Brazil wanted to create a bee that produced more honey than the native bees did. European honeybees produce lots of honey, but they can't live in a tropical environment like that found in Brazil. So in 1956 a geneticist brought queen bees from an African species to Brazil to crossbreed them with native honeybees. (Genetic engineering wasn't an option at that time.) The next year, twenty-six African queens and swarms of European worker bees escaped and crossbred in the wild to produce hybrids called Africanized honeybees. Unfortunately, the hybrid bees inherited the aggressive traits of the African bees instead of the milder temperament of European bees. The aggressive hybrids became known as "killer bees" because they attack people and animals far more vigorously than European honeybees do. The Africanized bees have gradually spread northward through South America and Central America and into the United States.

Even in controlled laboratories, science experiments can turn out all wrong. In 2001 researchers in Australia were trying to genetically engineer a contraceptive for mice. Instead, they accidentally created a disease that was so deadly it killed the mice instead of just keeping them from reproducing.

Africanized honeybees (right) *are a hybrid of African and European honeybees. Called "killer bees," Africanized bees are more aggressive than European honeybees.*

A USDA inspector checks a test plot of genetically modified corn. Critics argue that the USDA and other U.S. government agencies are not doing enough to regulate genetically modified plants and animals.

BIOTECH REGULATORS

In the United States, the products of biotechnology research are monitored by the U.S. Department of Agriculture (USDA), the Food and Drug Administration (FDA), the Environmental Protection Agency (EPA), and the National Institutes of Health (NIH). Each of these agencies plays a specific role in the regulation of new biotech products that enter the market for human use and consumption.

The President's Council on Bioethics was organized in 2001. It is composed of as many as eighteen leading scientists, doctors, ethicists, social scientists, lawyers, and theologians. The council informs the president and the nation of current developments in the field of biotechnology. The council also evaluates the ethical implications of controversial scientific research, including stem cell research and cloning.

PEOPLE IN THE BIOTECHNOLOGY FIELD

Biotechnology is a $39.2 billion industry employing an estimated 200,000 people in specialties including research and development, management, sales and marketing, regulation, biotech law, and public relations. Ethicists, entrepreneurs, activists, and lobbyists are also integral to the field of biotechnology.

Scientists who work in research and development conduct experiments and create new products. It usually takes ten or more years of research and half a billion dollars to develop a new product. To become a biotechnology researcher, students begin with a bachelor of science degree in chemistry, biology, microbiology, biochemistry, genetics, botany, zoology, or biotechnology. They usually continue their studies in graduate school.

Scientists who want to pursue a career in the field of biotechnology can work for universities or corporations. Some leading companies in the field of biotechnology include Monsanto, Genentech, and Advanced Cell Technology (ACT).

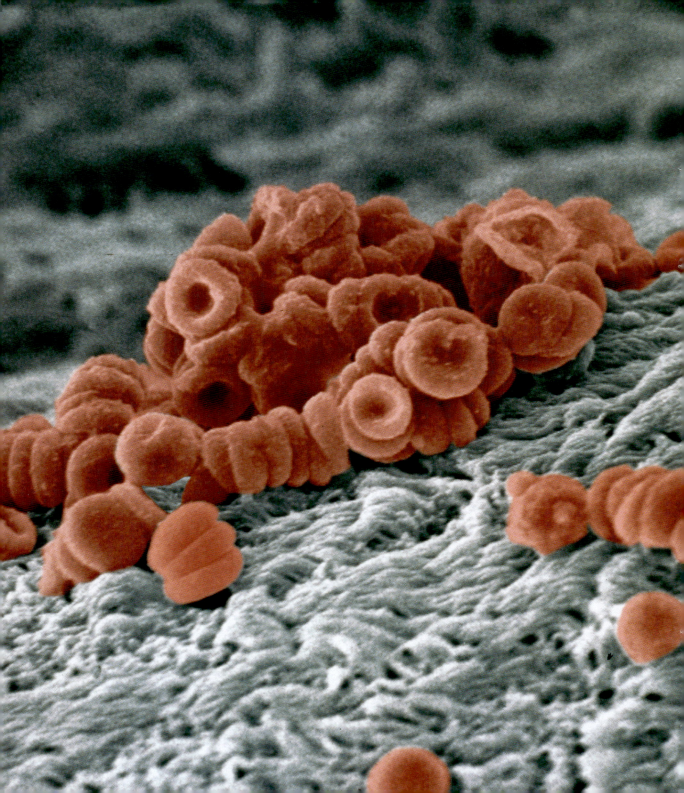

Chapter 2

GENETICS UNDER THE MICROSCOPE

Scientists could not see plant and animal cells until the microscope was invented around 1600. After that, it took centuries for scientists to understand the parts of cells and how they function in plants and in animals. Genetics was born in the early 1900s from the understanding of cells and the principles of heredity.

The word *genetics* is derived from the Greek word *genos,* which means "birth," and the Latin word *genus,* which means "race." Genetics is the study of heredity, or how physical characteristics are passed from generation to generation.

THE HISTORY OF GENETICS

Since ancient times, humans have tried to understand why we inherit certain traits and look the way we do. In the fourth century B.C., Hippocrates, a Greek physician who is considered the father of medicine, introduced the particulate theory. He postulated that every organ in the parents' bodies was represented as concentrated particles in the father's sperm and the mother's egg cells and the particles were passed on to the child. According to this theory, as the body changed through life, the characteristics passed on to children would also change.

Opposite: *A microscopic view of human red blood cells along an artery (blood vessel) wall. Powerful modern microscopes allow scientists to peer inside cells.*

If a parent's finger were cut off in an accident, a child conceived after the accident would be born missing a finger.

Aristotle, a student of Hippocrates, observed that traits acquired during a lifetime were not passed on to offspring. Parents with missing fingers had children with a full set of fingers. Aristotle proposed that a man's semen was formed from blood, and it produced "vital heat" that cooked and shaped a woman's menstrual blood into a child. This theory led to the expressions "bloodline" and "blood relative." Aristotle's theory was rejected, however. Variations of Hippocrates' particulate theory persisted for centuries.

In the 1600s, some scientists proposed a new theory: preformation. They believed that fully formed miniature individuals existed in a man's semen or in a woman's eggs. They believed this so strongly that they published drawings of "preformed" individuals they believed they had seen under the microscope. Discoveries by later scientists disproved this theory. The people that the preformation advocates drew were just figments of their imaginations.

Over the centuries, scientists modified and renamed the particulate theories. In the 1800s, French biologist Jean-Baptiste Lamarck called his particulate theory the inheritance of acquired characteristics. Charles Darwin, a British naturalist and author of *The Origin of Species*, called it pangenesis.

Gregor Mendel, an Austrian monk, figured out the principles of heredity by conducting experiments in breeding using pea plants. He meticulously recorded and analyzed the results. In 1866 he published a scientific paper titled *Experiments in Plant Hybridization*. His conclusions were a major breakthrough, but they were ignored by the scientific community during his lifetime. In 1900 Mendel's ideas were rediscovered.

Austrian monk and biologist Gregor Mendel examines one of his pea plants in 1860. Mendel's experiments with pea plants produced a greater under-standing of genetically inherited traits and provided a foundation for modern genetics and biotechnology.

He eventually became recognized as the father of genetics. The other theories proposed over the centuries were, in the end, rejected.

THE BASICS OF GENETICS

Understanding genetics begins with understanding the parts and functions of cells—the fundamental structural units of life. All plants and animals are made up of cells. Cells can work together as part of a tissue or organ, or they can work independently. Some entire living organisms are made up of just one cell. Other organisms are made up of millions of cells working together.

Animal cells are surrounded by a protein membrane that protects the contents of the cell. Plant cells have both a cell membrane and a rigid cell wall. Inside each cell are a variety of structures called organelles that carry out specific functions to help the cell survive.

A nucleus is located near the center of each plant or animal cell. The nucleus contains hereditary information coded in a molecule called deoxyribonucleic acid (DNA). The DNA molecule looks like a spiral staircase. DNA is tightly coiled in units called chromosomes. Humans have forty-six chromosomes. Half of these chromosomes are inherited from the mother and half from the father.

Bacterial cells, on the other hand, do not contain a nucleus. They typically have a single circular chromosome. They also have plasmids, which are smaller rings of DNA.

Segments of DNA are called genes. A gene is a unit of information. Each gene carries instructions for how to make specific protein molecules. Proteins are the building blocks of all living organisms. Next to water molecules, protein molecules are the most abundant in the human body. Proteins provide body structure and cell, tissue, and organ function.

Genes or collections of genes determine all of an organism's inherited traits, such as blue eyes or freckles. Each gene comes in variations called alleles. Mendel discovered that each allele is either dominant or recessive. A dominant allele is always expressed in the offspring. Recessive alleles are expressed only when the same allele is passed on by both parents. If an offspring receives a recessive allele from only one parent, the trait associated with that allele will not be present in the offspring. But the allele is still contained in the offspring's DNA, so it can be passed on to the next generation. In this case, the offspring is said to be a carrier of the recessive allele.

DNA'S PLACE IN CELLS

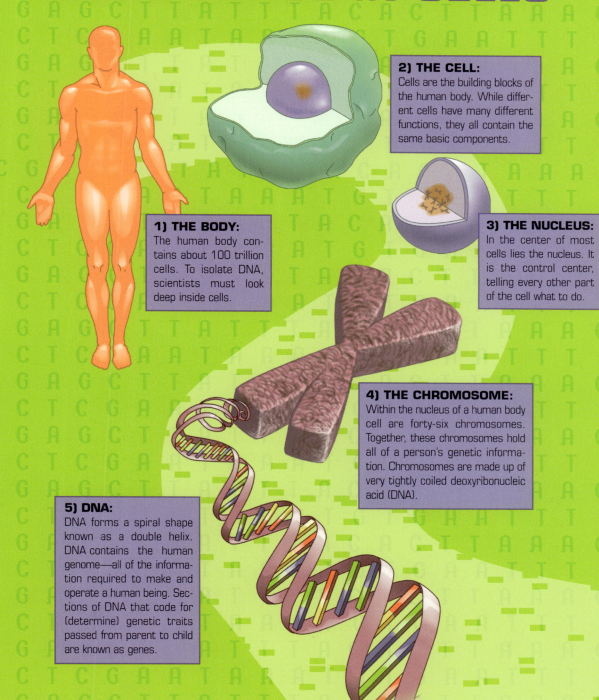

2) THE CELL:
Cells are the building blocks of the human body. While different cells have many different functions, they all contain the same basic components.

1) THE BODY:
The human body contains about 100 trillion cells. To isolate DNA, scientists must look deep inside cells.

3) THE NUCLEUS:
In the center of most cells lies the nucleus. It is the control center, telling every other part of the cell what to do.

4) THE CHROMOSOME:
Within the nucleus of a human body cell are forty-six chromosomes. Together, these chromosomes hold all of a person's genetic information. Chromosomes are made up of very tightly coiled deoxyribonucleic acid (DNA).

5) DNA:
DNA forms a spiral shape known as a double helix. DNA contains the human genome—all of the information required to make and operate a human being. Sections of DNA that code for (determine) genetic traits passed from parent to child are known as genes.

These frogs show harmful mutations. Recent studies of the frogs and others suggest these deformities may be a result of farm chemicals and parasitic infection (parasites feed off host organisms).

MUTATIONS

Mutations are changes in genes. Many mutations have environmental causes, such as exposure to radiation or to chemicals. The causes of some other mutations are unknown.

We are born with hundreds of genetic mutations that were passed on by our parents. During our lifetime, about thirty more mutations will occur within our genes. Most mutations never express themselves, so they have no effect on us.

But occasionally an expressed mutation is beneficial to an organism, helping it to better survive in its environment. A beneficial mutation increases the likelihood that an organism will live long enough to reproduce and pass the mutation on to its offspring. Over many generations, inherited beneficial mutations can help species adapt to changes in their environments.

But most expressed mutations cause harmful diseases and malformations. In the summer of 1995 in Henderson, Minnesota, a boy on a class field trip caught a frog like none he had ever seen before. Soon he and his classmates had caught several other frogs that all had severe deformities such as extra legs or missing or malformed eyes. Over the previous twenty years, David Hoppe, a scientist from the University of Minnesota, had examined thousands of frogs and found only two with abnormalities. But in 1996, he found more than two *hundred*. That same year, Richard Levey and a team of scientists from the Vermont Agency for Natural Resources reported an outbreak of frog deformities in Lake Champlain that were similar to those found in Minnesota.

Frogs are considered "bio-indicators," meaning that their general health is closely related to the health of the environment. Harmful chemicals such as herbicides and pesticides are washed off the land into lakes, wetlands, rivers, and streams. Once there, they can be absorbed through a frog's skin and enter its bloodstream. Such pollutants are considered a primary cause of frog mutations. Another significant contributor is increased ultraviolet radiation from the sun. Earth's atmosphere contains a gas called ozone that blocks harmful radiation. But the ozone layer has been depleted by humans' release of chemicals such as chlorofluorocarbons (CFCs) into the atmosphere.

CELL DIVISION

New cells are produced through a process called cell division. When a cell divides, it becomes two identical new cells. Cells are constantly dividing within every organism. For example, every fifteen to thirty days, the human body produces enough new skin cells through cell division to replace its entire covering of skin.

The process of cell division undergone by most cells is called mitosis. Reproductive cells (eggs and sperm) divide by a different method called meiosis. These cells have only half the number of chromosomes in body cells. Each human egg or sperm cell has twenty-three chromosomes. During fertilization, the father's sperm cell combines with the mother's egg to produce a cell called a zygote. The zygote has a full set of forty-six chromosomes. This single cell immediately begins to divide, and the zygote becomes a developing embryo.

Sometimes a zygote splits into two identical halves shortly after fertilization. Each half develops into a separate embryo, resulting in identical twins. Identical twins have exactly the same DNA, so they look alike.

THE STRUCTURE OF DNA

In 1944 Oswald Avery, Colin MacLeod, and Maclyn McCarty proved that DNA is responsible for carrying genetic traits in all organisms. In 1952 British molecular biologist Rosalind Franklin took a series of X-ray photographs of DNA. In January 1953, American biologist James Watson saw Franklin's best image, Photograph 51. He and British chemist Francis Crick used it to figure out that the DNA molecule is shaped like a twisted ladder or spiral staircase. This shape is called a double helix. *Helix* means spiral.

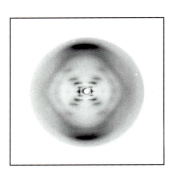

Franklin's Photograph 51 of the DNA molecule

The units that make up DNA are called nucleotides. Each nucleotide has three parts:

THE MOLECULAR STRUCTURE OF DNA

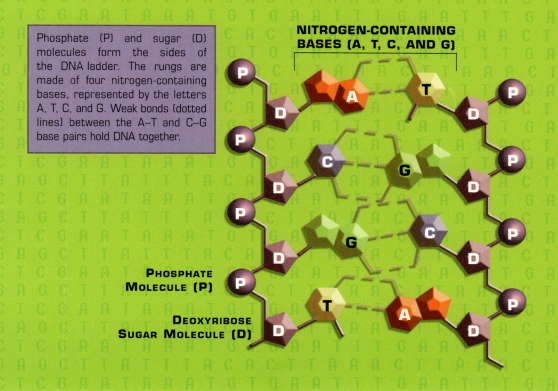

Phosphate (P) and sugar (D) molecules form the sides of the DNA ladder. The rungs are made of four nitrogen-containing bases, represented by the letters A, T, C, and G. Weak bonds (dotted lines) between the A–T and C–G base pairs hold DNA together.

NITROGEN-CONTAINING BASES (A, T, C, AND G)

PHOSPHATE MOLECULE (P)

DEOXYRIBOSE SUGAR MOLECULE (D)

a sugar molecule, a phosphate group, and a nitrogen-containing base. There are four different bases: adenine (A), thymine (T), cytosine (C), and guanine (G). A always bonds to T, and C always bonds to G. These base pairs form the steps in the DNA ladder. The sugar and phosphate molecules form the sides of the ladder.

Chemists are able to split molecules apart and combine them in different ways. Knowing that the DNA molecule is the basis of inheritance opened up the possibility of genetic engineering— manipulating the genetic material of an organism in the laboratory.

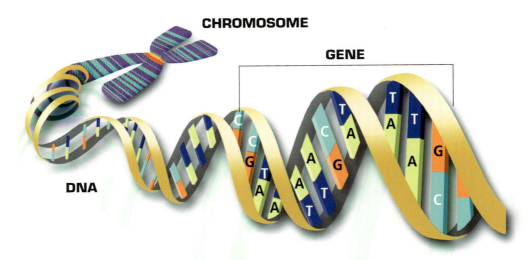

This illustration shows a gene, or a sequence of base pairs. Using chemical "scissors," scientists are able to cut genes from one DNA sample and splice them into another DNA sample.

SPLICING GENES

In 1973 American scientists Stanley Cohen and Herbert Boyer figured out a way to take DNA from one organism and incorporate it into another organism. They started with bacteria, since they are simple life-forms with a simple DNA structure. Bacteria contain one ring-shaped chromosome and free-floating plasmid rings. By using an enzyme (a biological molecule that helps chemical reactions take place) that acts like scissors to cut apart DNA, they could remove a piece of DNA from a plasmid, leaving an opening in the ring.

The scientists snipped some DNA from the plasmids of bacteria that could be killed by the antibiotics tetracycline and kanamycin. Then they took bits of DNA from bacteria that were resistant to tetracycline and from bacteria that were resistant to kanamycin. They attached these bits of DNA to the cut plasmids of the original bacteria, filling in the gap in the rings. To attach the new sections, they used an enzyme called ligase, which acts like DNA glue.

The antibiotics tetracycline and kanamycin were added to the container with the genetically engineered bacteria. The bacteria did not die. This was the beginning of genetic engineering, which is also called recombinant DNA (rDNA) technology.

Cohen and Boyer also tried a similar experiment, pasting a gene from a toad into *E. coli* bacteria. They wanted to know if the DNA of unrelated species could be combined. The experiment was successful. It opened the floodgates for all kinds of genetic engineering possibilities.

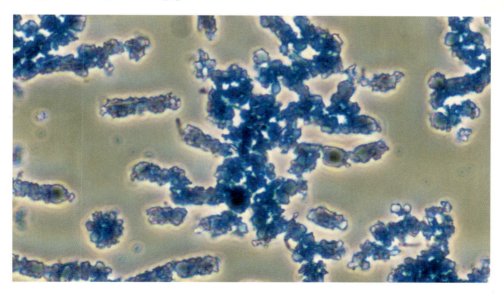

A microscopic view of genetically modified E. coli *bacteria. Scientists altered the DNA of this* E. coli *to produce the dark blue coloring.*

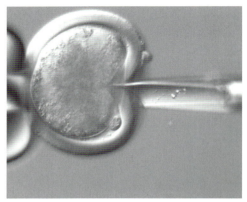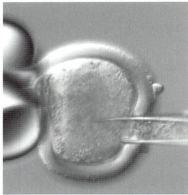

During enucleation, a fine needle is inserted into a cell (left), *and then the nucleus is removed* (right). *Enucleation makes cloning possible.*

CLONING

Cloning—creating identical copies of organisms—is an important tool in the field of biotechnology. Once an organism has been genetically modified, scientists can clone the new organism to make identical copies of it. The first cloned animal, a toad, was produced in 1952. In 1997 Scottish scientist Ian Wilmut succeeded in creating the first clone of an adult mammal. The offspring was a sheep named Dolly.

Wilmut and his team used three different sheep to create Dolly. They started with an egg cell from a Scottish Blackface sheep. They enucleated the egg cell (removed its nucleus), thereby removing the Scottish Blackface DNA. Next, they extracted the nucleus from a mammary gland (milk-producing organ) cell of a Finn Dorset sheep. The Finn Dorset nucleus and the enucleated Scottish Blackface egg cell were placed together in a petri dish. Electrical pulses were used to fuse the two cells into one cell containing Finn Dorset DNA.

THE CLONING OF DOLLY

FINN DORSET CELL DONOR (SHEEP TO BE CLONED)

SCOTTISH BLACKFACE EWE (EGG DONOR)

BODY CELL

EGG CELL

ENUCLEATION (REMOVAL OF BODY CELL NUCLEUS)

ENUCLEATION (REMOVAL OF EGG CELL NUCLEUS)

FINN DORSET CELL NUCLEUS FUSED INTO SCOTTISH BLACKFACE EGG CELL WITH ELECTRICITY

EMBRYO IMPLANTED INTO SURROGATE SCOTTISH BLACKFACE EWE'S UTERUS

FIVE MONTHS LATER DOLLY, A CLONED FINN DORSET LAMB, IS BORN

In nature, when an egg cell is fertilized, it causes a burst of energy that begins the process of cell division. The electrical impulse used in the laboratory caused the newly created egg cell to start dividing and become an embryo. After about a week, the embryo was implanted into a surrogate mother, a second Scottish Blackface sheep. Five months later, Dolly, a Finn Dorset sheep, was born.

THE HUMAN GENOME PROJECT

A genome is the complete genetic material of an organism—all of the information needed to make that organism and keep it alive. The human genome is made up of more than twenty thousand genes.

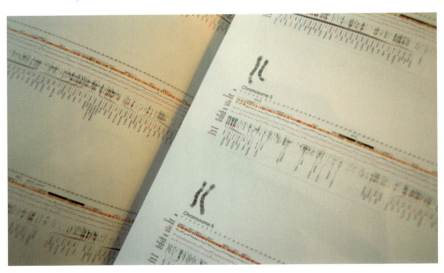

Made possible by the Human Genome Project, this portion of the human genome map shows the genes on human chromosomes 5 and 6 (the curvy black lines at center).

In 1990 scientists began mapping the human genome, figuring out where the genes are located on each chromosome. The project was completed in 2003. Scientists have also mapped the rat, mouse, dog, and chimpanzee genomes. They have chosen eighteen more genomes to map, including those of orangutans, elephants, and cats.

It is anticipated that scientists will be able to use the human genome map to gain a better understanding of genetic diseases such as cystic fibrosis, which are passed from generation to generation. They hope the new information will help them to develop more effective ways to diagnose and treat—and even prevent—genetic disorders.

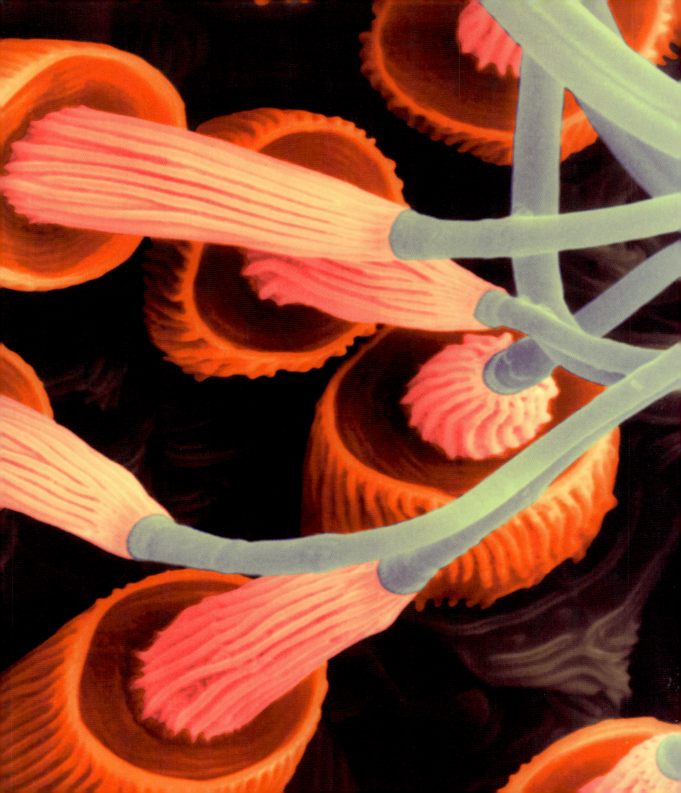

Chapter 3

ANIMAL ODDITIES

A goat that produces spider silk in its milk may sound like a creature from another planet, but it is just one of the many genetically altered animals that scientists have created. Scientists have genetically altered animals such as cows, goats, and pigs to make them produce pharmaceutical drugs or nonmedicinal products in their milk, blood, eggs, and semen. Such animals are referred to as "pharm" animals.

Nexia Biotechnologies has patented a process allowing them to transfer a spider gene that codes for a silk protein into a goat's mammary cells. Surprisingly, a spider's silk gland and a goat's mammary gland are anatomically similar. The goat's milk looks and tastes the same, but scientists can extract silk proteins from it.

Biotech companies don't use spiders to make spider silk because they are hard to control and the process would be too inefficient. A large number of spiders would be needed, and they would have to be separated to keep them from eating one another. "It's like trying to farm tigers. You put ten thousand spiders in a room and come back a week later and there's one big happy spider left," said Jeffrey Turner, chief executive officer (CEO) of Nexia Biotechnologies.

Why would scientists want to create spider silk? Because spider silk is one of the strongest materials known—it is ten times stronger than steel. But it is also very flexible. A silk cable as thick as a human thumb could hold the weight of a jumbo jet.

Opposite: *A microscopic view of a spider's silk glands*

Transgenic plants and animals, such as these goats from Nexia Biotechnologies, often look no different than natural organisms. The amazing changes are at the genetic level, undetectable to the human eye. These Nexia goats produce a protein that breaks down nerve agents (chemical weapons).

Silk also is light enough and strong enough to make bulletproof vests. It can also be made into artificial tendons or used as sutures to stitch wounds.

Not everyone is pleased about the engineering of goats as factories to produce silk, however. The animal rights organization People for the Ethical Treatment of Animals opposes the production of pharm animals. "Goats are not test tubes with whiskers," said Mary Beth Sweetland, director of research and investigation at PETA.

CLOT-BUSTING GOATS

Goats are also being genetically altered to produce the human protein antithrombin III, which dissolves blood clots. It is given to some patients who are undergoing heart surgery to prevent potentially deadly blood clots from forming.

Genzyme Transgenics has successfully cloned clot-busting goats. Cloning is more cost-effective than genetically altering many goat embryos, waiting for these goats to be born, and then breeding them. Traditional breeding of transgenic goats takes longer than cloning, and there's no guarantee that the goats' offspring will have the genetic traits needed to produce the medicine.

FAST-GROWING SALMON

Some pharm animals have been developed to increase food production. One of the more successful transgenic experiments involves the Atlantic salmon. It began when scientist Choy Hew accidentally froze a tank full of flounder. Hew was surprised to find that the fish were still alive after the tank was thawed.

Hew learned that fish living in frigid polar waters produce a natural antifreeze. The gene that produces the antifreeze protein turns on only when the fish are exposed to extremely cold temperatures, allowing the fish to survive. But one section of the antifreeze gene acts like a switch that is always turned on.

In the wild, Atlantic salmon grow only during the summer. Their growth hormone gene is turned off in the winter. Hew and his colleague Garth Fletcher theorized that if the antifreeze gene were coupled with the chinook salmon growth hormone gene and inserted into Atlantic salmon eggs, the genetically modified fish would grow at an accelerated rate. This combination of genes resulted in a genetically modified salmon that produces the growth hormone continuously, not just during the summer, so the salmon grow twice as fast. Farmers are able to raise more salmon in less time, with lower feed costs. Consumers could benefit because the price of salmon would tend to decrease as the supply increased.

Although the GM salmon are being raised for food, the FDA has classified them as a drug because the transferred gene functions as an animal drug. This classification forces farmers who grow transgenic salmon to meet specific safety requirements to protect the humans who will be eating the fish.

Farmers take precautions when raising genetically altered salmon, but some people believe that the transgenic fish pose a threat to the environment. The genetically modified salmon are larger than and reach sexual maturity sooner than wild salmon. If transgenic salmon got loose, they would have a breeding advantage over the smaller, nontransgenic salmon. Ultimately, the nontransgenic salmon could become extinct. The salmon farmers argue that they can raise the genetically modified salmon in closed aquariums to prevent escapes. They also could create sterile salmon that would be unable to breed with nontransgenic salmon even if they did get loose.

"ENVIROPIGS"

The goal of reducing pollution motivated scientists at the University of Guelph (Ontario, Canada) to genetically alter pigs to create animals they call "Enviropigs." Pigs are normally unable to digest phytate phosphorus, the type of phosphorus found in the grain they eat. Since the pigs can't digest the phosphorus, it comes out in their manure. Pig manure is used to fertilize farm fields. Rain carries phosphorus from the pigs' manure into ponds, streams, and rivers. Phosphorus promotes the growth of algae, which in turn reduces the amount of oxygen in the water. Then fish and other aquatic life die.

The Guelph researchers engineered pigs whose saliva contained phytase, the enzyme that breaks down phytate phosphorus, with the goal of making the pigs' manure more environmentally friendly. Scientists combined a phytase-producing gene from the *E. coli* bacterium with a mouse gene that instructs the salivary glands to produce a protein. The combination of genes was inserted into the nucleus of a one-celled pig embryo, which was then implanted into a surrogate pig.

Three genetically engineered pigs were produced by this method. The scientists named them Wayne, Jacques, and Gordie, after Canadian hockey players. These pigs' manure contained 56 to 75 percent less phosphorus than manure from nontransgenic pigs.

Debate surrounds the GM pigs. For example, environmental groups such as the Sierra Club and Greenpeace are opposed to breeding them. Opponents believe that farmers' current practice of adding the phytase enzyme to the grain their pigs eat is effective enough and genetic modification is unnecessary. Also, a new strain of corn that contains the phytase enzyme could be used as an alternative feed ingredient.

Researchers at the University of Guelph (Ontario, Canada) have genetically altered pig DNA to create pigs that produce less phosphorus in their manure than normal pigs do.

The phytase corn has been shown to reduce phosphorus in pigs' manure by 50 percent.

Undeterred by the critics, the scientists plan to test the engineered pigs for abnormalities. They hope to market them in the next few years.

CLONING FARM ANIMALS

All types of farm animals are being cloned—everything from sheep and goats to cows. Texas A&M University is a leader in animal cloning. Researchers at Texas A&M were the first to clone a bull for its resistance to brucellosis, tuberculosis, and salmonellosis—infectious bacterial diseases that can spread among animals and humans. These diseases are not much of a problem in the United States or Canada. But they are an issue in countries such as Mexico, despite vaccinations, testing, quarantine, and the practice of killing infected animals. Imported livestock could possibly cause new outbreaks in the United States.

The disease-resistant bull's name was Bull 86. Researchers froze cells from the tip of Bull 86's ear in 1985. Fifteen years later—three years after the death of Bull 86—scientists used the frozen cells to create a clone named Bull 86 Squared. DNA analysis showed that Bull 86 Squared is an exact copy of Bull 86.

"The impact of cloning disease-resistant cattle is potentially monumental," said Garry Adams, a scientist at Texas A&M University. "For example, in countries where they are unable to pasteurize milk to kill the bacteria or process meat appropriately, breeding disease-resistant cows could greatly contribute to a safer food supply."

Engineering livestock for disease resistance is not a permanent solution, however. Due to their rapid rate of reproduction, bacteria change quickly in response to environmental conditions, giving rise to new strains of disease. While it might be possible to reduce the negative effects of specific strains, disease would not be eliminated.

INHERITED TRAITS OF CLONES

Ralph and Sandra Fisher were the owners of a twenty-one-year-old bull named Chance. They asked Texas A&M to clone Chance because he was sterile and they wanted another bull with Chance's gentle disposition. The scientists had to try 189 times before succeeding in cloning the bull. A few months after Chance died, his clone, Second Chance, was born.

Since Chance was an old bull, Second Chance may be physically old even though he is young in chronological age. This phenomenon was first observed in Dolly, the first cloned adult sheep. At the ends of the chromosomes are segments of DNA called telomeres. These segments do not contain genes. When a cell divides, the DNA in each chromosome is copied. During this process, some of each telomere is lost. But the chromosome's genetic material stays intact. As an organism ages and its DNA is copied over and over, the telomeres shrink. When they become too short, the cell dies. Since the cells used to clone Dolly were from an adult sheep, their telomeres were short and so were Dolly's. Even though Dolly was chronologically a newborn, her short telomeres made her genetically older.

Scientists also want to study the physical and behavioral similarities between the cloned bull and the original bull. The owners of Second Chance say that not only is he the identical image of Chance, but his personality is the same.

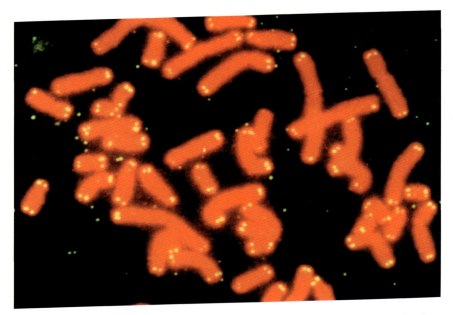

Stained chromosomes reveal yellow highlighted telomeres at their tips. Telomeres protect chromosomes from damage, but they erode as an organism ages.

"The day we brought Second Chance home, he laid in the same exact spot [where Chance would lie]. And the first time he saw Ralph, he loped across the pasture toward him, licking his face and his boots," said Sandra Fisher. "I'm a little hesitant to say he has a memory, but he has the same instincts. Let me put it like this: Given the same problem, Chance and Second Chance would figure it out the same way."

Scientists say not enough clones exist to draw any definite conclusions about behavior. But the Texas A&M cloning that produced two piglets named Big Bertha and Tiny Tina resulted in some interesting observations. One major difference between pigs and animals such as sheep and cattle is that pigs give birth to more than one offspring at a time (a litter), while sheep and cattle generally give birth to only one offspring. Even though Big Bertha and Tiny Tina are littermates with identical genes, their bodies are different sizes. Their personalities are also different. Tiny Tina is the smallest of the litter, and she is nervous. Big Bertha is 40 percent larger than Tiny Tina, and she is more aggressive. Scientists are still trying to figure out why such differences occur. They believe that the environment affects personality and physical development.

Researchers in Japan are studying re-cloning—the cloning of clones. The first bull that was a clone of a clone was born in January 2000 at the Kagoshima Prefectural Cattle Breeding Development Institute. Japan sends cloned cattle to market for human consumption. They consider cloned cattle identical twins. If a certain bull produces good meat, they want to be able to use that bull time after time. The researchers are interested in possible abnormalities, specifically in the aging process, of a bull that is a clone of a clone.

The process of re-cloning is the same as cloning. To clone a clone, the scientists took cells from a cloned bull's ear and fused them with enucleated egg cells. The eggs were then implanted into surrogate cows.

Cloning of farm animals is common. But some people oppose the procedure, saying it is morally wrong. These people argue that too many failed attempts precede each successful cloning, too many deaths occur during the gestation period, and too many deformed offspring are born. Researchers themselves have noted that even if an animal is born with no abnormalities, abnormalities may occur later in the animal's life.

FRANKENBUGS

For every acre on earth, there are about 14 pounds (6.4 kg) of people and around 400 pounds (nearly 200 kg) of insects.

The world's 2,500 different types of mosquitoes carry a variety of contagious diseases. Many, such as yellow fever, dengue fever, and malaria, are deadly to humans.

Fever, chills, aches, pains, vomiting, convulsions, and coma are the symptoms of malaria. The disease kills 1 million people out of the 300 to 500 million cases reported each year. Malaria kills more humans than any other contagious disease except tuberculosis. Even though malaria may be treatable if it's caught in time, a child dies from the disease every forty seconds.

Malaria is caused by a parasite that is carried by mosquitoes. When a malaria-carrying mosquito bites a human, that person gets infected. Ordinarily, once a person has been ill with a disease, such as chicken pox, the body creates antibodies to fight it and builds up immunity so that person won't catch the disease again. Vaccines work in a similar way—they cause the body to produce antibodies to a disease. But malaria survivors don't necessarily become immune to the disease—they can have it over and over—so developing an effective malaria vaccine is tricky.

Another problem with fighting malaria is that the parasite's DNA can mutate to resist drugs that are effective in killing it. The most deadly mutant strain of malaria is the *Plasmodium falciparum* parasite. This strain has appeared in Asia, South America, and Africa.

Some researchers have been trying to use pharm animals to create drug treatments for malaria. For instance, scientists have succeeded in genetically engineering mice that produce a malaria vaccine in their milk. The vaccine has been tested on monkeys and has been shown to protect them from malaria. However, it is years away from being ready for human use. The next step is to try to genetically alter larger animals, such as goats, to produce the vaccine in their milk. Once scientists figure out how to make the vaccine safe for humans, genetically altered goats may be able to produce enough medicine in their milk to immunize twenty million people a year.

Scientists have also succeeded in genetically modifying the *Anopheles* mosquito, the type of mosquito that carries the malaria parasite. Ultimately, researchers want to genetically alter the mosquito so that it will no longer carry the parasite. They are also working on genetically altering mosquitoes that carry West Nile disease, dengue fever, and yellow fever.

Releasing transgenic mosquitoes into the natural population is controversial, since controlling them would be impossible. Genetically engineered mosquitoes might mutate into something more harmful, or they might crossbreed with other insects, producing a "super-pest" that would cause deadly environmental and health problems.

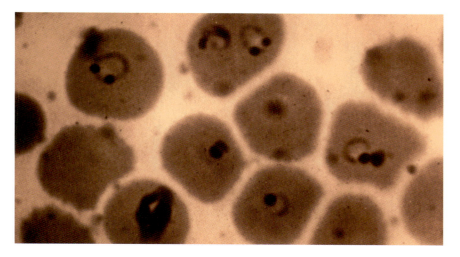

Human red blood cells infected with the Plasmodium falciparum *malaria parasite (dark shapes in cells). Genetically altered mice and the malaria-carrying* anopheles *mosquito could be the keys to eradicating the disease.*

Viruses

Viruses are the simplest of all life-forms. They consist of a protein shell surrounding a core of DNA. Viruses are so tiny that they can be seen only through the most powerful microscopes.

A virus reproduces by first attaching itself to a cell in a host organism. The virus then injects its DNA into the cell. The viral DNA instructs the host cell to replicate the viral DNA and assemble many copies of the virus. Finally, the cell explodes, releasing the new viruses, which go on to infect other cells.

Scientists have learned how to use viruses as vectors. A vector is a means of moving genes from one organism to another. Genes that code for desired proteins are added to a virus's DNA. The viral DNA is also altered to prevent the virus from reproducing. Then the virus is introduced into another organism. When the virus injects its modified DNA into the organism's cells, it delivers the new genes.

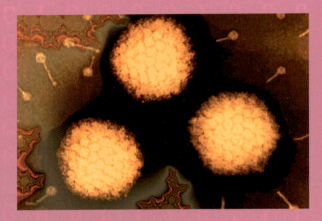

Three adenoviruses, members of a group of viruses that cause colds and other mild diseases in humans. Scientists often use adenoviruses as genetic vectors.

CATERPILLAR FACTORY

Scientists have discovered that caterpillars, specifically the cabbage looper moth caterpillar, produce a protein that can be used in vaccinations for animals such as chickens and fish. The protein can also be used as a detector of anthrax and smallpox, diseases that could be used in biological warfare.

To harvest the caterpillar protein, scientists at Chesapeake PERL have developed a larva factory. The assembly line begins by placing cabbage looper eggs in separate compartments of plastic containers. The eggs are incubated for seven days, and then scientists insert a virus into each egg.

The virus contains foreign genes, including the green fluorescent protein gene that makes jellyfish glow. When the larvae have produced the desired protein, they glow, so the scientists know they are ready to be harvested. The glowing larvae are dumped into a machine that grinds them up into a liquid. The protein is then extracted from the liquid.

Scientists aren't concerned about the caterpillars getting loose in the wild and interbreeding there. The inserted virus makes the caterpillars sterile and ultimately kills them.

BIOTECH PETS

Genetic engineers are trying to alter the genetic makeup of cats and dogs for various traits including longer lives, nonshedding hair, and interesting colors. ALLERCA is a company that is working on genetically altering cats so they won't make people who are allergic to ordinary cats sneeze or break out in hives.

Scientists isolated the gene that makes the protein Fel d1, which keeps a cat's skin moist but also causes allergic reactions in some people. To make an allergen-free cat, scientists take some cells from a cat's skin and grow them in a test tube. Then scientists "knock out," or delete, the gene that makes the Fel d1 protein and replace it with a defective gene. The cells are fused with enucleated egg cells. Once the cells develop into embryos, they are inserted into a surrogate cat. The resulting kittens would not produce Fel d1, thereby making them allergen-free.

Once an allergen-free cat has been created, scientists will try to reproduce it, both by cloning and by the traditional method of breeding. Although an unmodified cat was successfully cloned in 2001, it is difficult to do so. Another potential problem is that knocking out the gene that makes protein Fel d1 may prove to have a harmful effect on the cat.

Even though pet cloning has yet to become common, Genetic Savings and Clone produced the first clone of a deceased pet, a cat named Little Nicky, in 2004. That year, the company also was at work creating the first clone of a pet dog. Canine Cryobank and others offer pet cell banking. With the hope that cloning of pets will be easy and affordable in the future, owners send pet cell samples to Canine Cryobank, where technicians freeze and store them for a fee.

At Texas A&M University, scientists are working on the Missyplicity Project. The owners of a dog named Missy are paying millions of dollars to have scientists try to clone their beloved canine. Cell samples were taken from Missy's lip and belly, then grown in a culture and frozen. Scientists hope to learn how to clone a dog, while also gaining a better understanding of the canine reproductive system. Even if the scientists are successful in cloning Missy, she will not be Missy reincarnated. The cloned Missy will be a genetically identical twin who may or may not act like the original Missy.

How Much Is That Human-Made Animal?

In the future, you may be able to go into a pet store and see a sign for human-made animals, such as a green-glowing monkey or a blue dog. Be prepared to pay a hefty price for them.

Regular puppy from the dog pound	$65–95
Cloned puppy	$2.2–3.7 million (first batch)
Regular monkey	$3,700
Green-glowing monkey	$300,000 (first batch)
Regular mouse	$1.70
Green-glowing mouse	$170
Made-to-order transgenic mouse	$35,000
Regular farm goat	$700–1,400
Human-made pharm goat	$100,000
Regular kitten from the pound	$65–95
Allergen-free kitten	$750–1,000

GloFish, as their name suggests, have been genetically altered to glow. The fish are the first genetically altered house pets.

Once scientists succeed in cloning a dog, they want to begin cloning service dogs such as Seeing Eye dogs, search-and-rescue dogs, and dogs used in pet therapy. Male service dogs are commonly neutered at a young age so they can focus on their work. Therefore, reproducing good service dogs can be difficult unless they are cloned.

"FROZEN ZOOS"

Will dinosaurs roam the earth again? The possibility of cloning extinct and endangered animals may become reality. In 1997 a family of reindeer herders in the Siberian tundra came across a woolly mammoth's tusk. It was soon discovered that the entire 6-ton (5-t) mammoth had been preserved in the frozen tundra for twenty to thirty thousand years. Paleontologist Larry Agenbroad and French explorer Bernard Buigues were part of the team that excavated the mammoth in a 23-ton (21-t) block of ice that was flown 220 miles (350 km) by helicopter to the ice cave that was their laboratory. The ice cave's temperature was a constant 7°F (-14°C). The scientists used hair dryers to gradually thaw the ice encasing the mammoth.

Scientists are trying to figure out why woolly mammoths became extinct. They are also going to try to clone the mammoth. But even though its body is intact, its DNA may be too old and deteriorated for cloning to be possible.

The cloning process would involve extracting DNA from the woolly mammoth and inserting it into the enucleated egg of an Asian elephant, a close living relative of the woolly mammoth. Once the egg developed into an embryo, it would be implanted into an Asian elephant that would be the woolly mammoth's surrogate mother.

The tusks of a complete woolly mammoth discovered in Siberia in 1997. Cloning may make it possible to create a living copy of the twenty-three-thousand-year-old animal.

Another extinct animal that scientists are trying to bring back to life by cloning is the huia bird, which once lived in the forests of New Zealand. The Maori people, who are native to New Zealand, used huia feathers in their ceremonial head-dresses. In the early 1900s, it was fashionable for European women to wear hats with huia feathers. The demand for feathers increased the killing of the bird. By the 1920s, it was extinct. In 1999 some New Zealand high school students organized a scientific conference to discuss the possibility of bringing the huia back from extinction. At the conference, researchers agreed to try to clone the huia. Scientists will have to examine the bones and tendons of preserved huia birds to try to find cells that can be used in cloning. They are years away from creating a clone.

One somewhat successful experiment was the cloning of a gaur, an endangered species of wild ox from Southeast Asia. Since the forests of Southeast Asia are decreasing in size and the gaur is hunted, its existence is threatened. The gaur is difficult to breed in zoos, so scientists at Advanced Cell Technology cloned a gaur by inserting its genetic material into an enucleated cow's egg. The egg was then implanted into a cow, which is physically similar to a gaur.

It took scientists one hundred tries to create a gaur embryo to implant into a cow. The cow carried the gaur to term. Two days after the birth, however, the baby gaur died of dysentery. The scientists don't think the dysentery was a result of the cloning. The surrogate cow's health was unaffected by the birthing.

Advanced Cell Technology wants to clone other endangered species, such as the bucardo, the gorilla, the ocelot, and the giant panda. The company also wants to store cells of endangered animals to create "frozen zoos" for cloning purposes.

Cells, embryos, and the genetic information that they contain can be stored nearly indefinitely in liquid nitrogen deep-freeze.

Some people oppose cloning endangered species. One argument is that the availability of cloned animals will cause people to become lax about conservation efforts, further reducing wild populations of endangered species.

GREEN-GLOWING RABBIT AS ART

Artist Eduardo Kac's goal is to combine technology and art in a way that causes people to become aware of and speak out about social issues. With this in mind, he collaborated with French scientist Louis-Marie Houdebine to produce a work of art. Houdebine created an albino rabbit whose DNA contained the jellyfish glow gene, GFP. The transgenic rabbit's name was Alba. Under ultraviolet light, Alba's living cells, including those in her eyes and inside her ears, glowed green.

Kac wanted to use Alba as part of his performance art. He also wanted to bring her into his home. To Kac, the social ramifications of integrating Alba into his family were part of his art. But the scientists would not allow Alba to leave the laboratory. One reason may have been the possibility that the rabbit would get loose and breed with other rabbits, thereby adding her transgenic genes to the rabbit population's gene pool.

Some animal rights activists consider it wrong to use transgenic animals as art, saying it serves no medical purpose and the animals may suffer. But Stuart A. Newman, a professor of cell biology and anatomy at New York Medical College, thinks the attention the art receives may have a positive effect. "It kind of turns the searchlight back on scientists," said Newman. "There are some pretty awfully deformed animals in transgenic research, and scientists have sometimes done things with no good theory behind it."

Chapter 4

ORGAN PHARMS

In 1984 a baby named Fae was born prematurely with a fatal heart disease. Baby Fae needed a new heart, but rarely are human infant hearts available for transplantation.

Dr. Leonard L. Bailey of the Loma Linda University Medical Center in California made the controversial proposal to replace Baby Fae's heart with the heart of a baboon. This type of transplant had been attempted on adults, but never on an infant. Baby Fae lived for almost three weeks after the baboon's heart was transplanted into her chest. An autopsy indicated that the baboon's blood type had not been compatible with Baby Fae's. The mismatch caused clotting to occur in her heart, killing her. This type of surgery has not been performed on an infant since.

XENOTRANSPLANTATION

When a doctor removes an organ from an animal, such as a baboon or pig, and transplants it into a human, the procedure is called xenotransplantation. *Xeno* means "foreign." The history of the procedure dates back to 1682, when a Russian aristocrat injured his skull. Bone was taken from a dog's skull and implanted in the man's head. As far as the doctors could tell, the xenotransplantation was successful. But church leaders were furious over the incident, so the dog's bone was removed.

Opposite: *An artist's representation of an organ farm. The technology to grow human organs is as exciting as it is controversial.*

Controversy still brews over the ethical issues of transplanting animal organs and parts into humans. The threat of introducing new, lethal viruses into the human population is one reason people are opposed to xenotransplants. Some scientists are concerned that viruses present in animal organs may be able to infect human cells. Even viruses that don't harm their animal hosts could be lethal to humans, possibly causing a deadly epidemic.

But animal cruelty is the main focus of the controversy. Animal rights activists argue that the pigs and primates used in xenotransplant research are not treated humanely. It is their opinion that it is morally wrong to sacrifice animals' lives in order to advance human medicine.

From 1995 to 2000, the British xenotransplant research company Imutran financed experiments conducted by Huntingdon Life Sciences involving pig-to-nonhuman primate transplants. More than 10,000 pigs, 420 monkeys, and an estimated 50 baboons were killed. The average post-transplant survival rate was thirteen days, but one baboon, named X201M, survived for thirty-nine days after his heart was removed and replaced with a genetically modified pig's heart.

In 2000 the research log that documented these experiments was leaked to Uncaged Campaigns, a British animal rights group. Uncaged Campaigns passed it on to the British newspaper *Daily Express*. The experiments outraged the public.

"One of the most unfortunate animals had a piglet heart transplanted into his neck," said Dan Lyons of Uncaged Campaigns. "For several days . . . the transplanted heart . . . was seeping pus as a result of infections that often occur in the wound site where the operation has taken place. He suffered from body tremors, vomiting, diarrhea. . . . I don't think the animal experiments can ever be justified because the deliberate

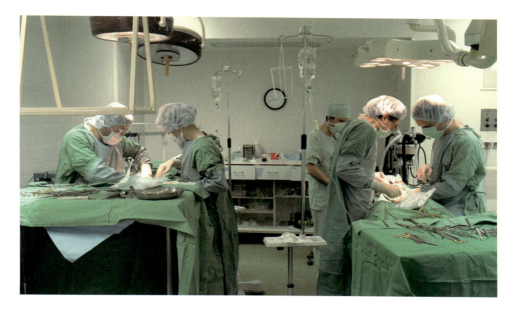

Scientists perform a xenotransplant of a pig's liver into a baboon in the late 1990s. Although highly controversial, cross-species transplants could provide the organs necessary to save human lives.

infliction of violence, suffering, and death on another is wrong, you know, be it a human or any kind of animal." Although many people found these experiments deplorable, scientists viewed them as a success because they provided valuable information that could be used to advance medicine.

People who have benefited from clinical trials (controlled research studies that evaluate medical treatments) involving pigs' organs don't have qualms about the controversy because these trials saved their lives. Scientists stand by their research methods, citing the shortage of human organs available for transplant and the dire circumstances patients who are waiting for an organ transplant must endure.

Each year in the United States, sixty to seventy thousand patients with heart problems need a heart transplant. But each year, only about two thousand of those patients receive a transplant due to the shortage of organs available. Scientists also point out that each year more than ninety million pigs are slaughtered for human consumption in the United States. "If you can use it for sausages and bacon, the question is why can't you use it to save a life?" said Robert P. Lanza, vice president of medical and scientific development at Advanced Cell Technology.

The main argument in favor of xenotransplants is the shortage of human organs available for transplantation. According to the United Network for Organ Sharing (UNOS), every thirteen minutes a person is added to the organ transplant waiting list and every ninety-one minutes someone on that waiting list dies because an organ didn't become available in time.

Both nonhuman primates and pigs have organs that are similar in size and structure to human organs. But pigs are considered a better option for xenotransplantation than nonhuman primates for a number of reasons. Because nonhuman primates are more closely related to humans than pigs are, nonhuman primates are more likely to carry viruses that can infect a transplant patient. An example is the monkey virus herpes 8, which can infect and kill a human in a few days. Pigs breed more quickly than primates and deliver more offspring. The offspring mature more quickly than primate offspring, so they can be used for transplantation sooner. Scientists must overcome two main obstacles, however, to make pig-to-human transplants successful.

The first problem in xenotransplantation of pig organs is hyperacute rejection. Pigs' tissues contain Gal, a type of sugar molecule, that is also present in certain dangerous bacteria, viruses, and parasites. The human body recognizes Gal as a sign that it has been invaded. It attacks the pig organ, cutting off its oxygen supply. The organ soon dies.

The second problem is that pig DNA contains porcine endogenous retroviruses (PERVs). The viruses don't harm pigs, but they can infect human cells, causing the body to immediately reject the pig organ. The possibility exists that PERVs could mutate into new viruses that are even more dangerous.

One recipient of a pig's organ was Rob Pennington, a twenty-year-old man whose liver was failing. The liver is the body's largest internal organ. Every minute about 3 pints (1.4 l) of blood pass through it. The liver takes nutrients from the blood for use by the rest of the body and gets rid of toxins. A functioning liver is necessary for life.

Time was running out for Rob, and no human livers were available. Doctors decided to use the liver of a pig named Wilbur.

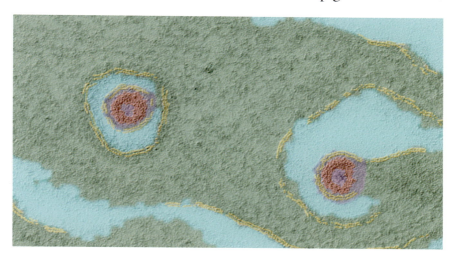

The porcine endogenous retrovirus, or PERV (red). PERV is a major concern in xenotransplantation from pigs to primates, including humans.

The idea wasn't to replace Rob's liver permanently with Wilbur's liver. Instead, the doctors wanted to give him more time as he waited for a human liver to become available. Wilbur's liver was connected to Rob's blood vessels but kept outside of his body. This is referred to as an *ex vivo* (outside the body) procedure. The pig's liver cleaned toxins out of Rob's blood for three days. By then a human liver was found and successfully transplanted into him. He recovered completely.

As the recipient of a xenotransplant, Rob must follow guidelines established by the FDA. Since scientists aren't sure what the long-term impact of the PERV viruses on human cells might be, xenotransplant patients are advised to practice safe sex and not to have children. They can't donate blood for transfusion into other people. Finally, they must donate their bodies to science when they die so researchers can investigate the effects of the xenotransplant.

Since hyperacute rejection and PERVs are major hurdles in moving forward with xenotransplants, scientists are trying to genetically engineer pigs to make their organs more compatible with the human body. One method involves "knocking out" undesirable genes. A pig gene called *GATA1* is responsible for the production of Gal. If this gene were removed from the pig's genome, Gal would no longer be present to cause the human body to reject the organ. Scientists have found that the pig genome includes two copies of the *GATA1* gene. They were able to knock out one copy of the *GATA1* gene in a pig's egg cell, then clone seven piglets from the egg. Three of the piglets died. Of the four surviving piglets, one was born with physical defects. It is unclear whether removing the *GATA1* gene will cause any long-term health problems for genetically engineered pigs. Scientists are trying to knock out both copies of the *GATA1* gene from the pig's genome. They hope this will reduce the risk of hyperacute rejection of pig organs.

Researchers are also working to overcome the PERV virus obstacle. They have found a type of miniature pig whose PERV virus doesn't seem to be able to enter human cells. The next step for the researchers is to transplant organs from these pigs into nonhuman primates, such as baboons, to see if the primates' bodies accept the transplanted organs.

GROWING HUMAN ORGANS IN THE LAB

In 1997 a 4-inch (10-cm) mouse grew a 3-inch (8-cm) third ear. The third ear wasn't on the mouse's head. The extra-long ear was growing on the mouse's back, and it wasn't a mouse ear— it was a fully developed human ear.

This experiment, conducted by Dr. Joseph Vacanti, helped propel the new field of "tissue engineering" into the limelight. Tissue engineering is the growing of human body parts in the laboratory. The process starts with the construction of a scaffold, a framework made from the same material as the dissolving sutures sometimes used to stitch together wounds. The scaffold is shaped like the desired human body part. Then the scaffold is covered with human stem cells.

Stem cells are special cells that are harvested from a patient's body or from an embryo. These cells are unique in that they are not specialized to perform a particular function. When a stem cell divides, each daughter cell can either remain a stem cell or become a cell with a more specialized function, such as a blood cell, a muscle cell, or a nerve cell. Stem cells replenish dying, damaged, and diseased cells in the body. Stem cells are practically immortal—they continue to divide into new cells indefinitely.

A Chicken with Four Legs

Scientists at the Salk Institute in La Jolla, California, transformed the wings of chicken embryos into legs. This feat was made possible by the discovery of the gene *Tbx4*, which is present in both humans and chickens. This gene instructs cells to develop into legs, rather than wings (in chickens) or arms (in humans).

The scientists used a virus to transport the *Tbx4* gene into the tissue in the wing areas of one-day-old chicken embryos. At this point, the embryos had not yet begun to develop wings or legs. By the following day, limbs had begun to form. The scientists moved them to the belly of the embryos to ensure that the limbs wouldn't receive genetic cues from other cells in the wing areas that had not been infected with the *Tbx4* gene. Otherwise, the limbs might have become wings anyway. The scientists found that most of the limbs developed into legs.

The goal of this research is to understand limb malformations, which are common birth defects in humans. It could also help in treating the rare disorder Holt-Oram syndrome, which causes people to have shorter-than-usual arms and hands.

The scaffolding and stem cells are placed in an incubator at human body temperature, 98.6°F (37°C). Nutrients and seed cells (specialized cells that guide the stem cell's development) are added, and the stem cells begin to divide. As the new tissue grows, the scaffolding begins to disintegrate, just as dissolving sutures do.

In January 1999, Dr. Anthony Atala created lab-grown bladders and transplanted them into six dogs. He had decided to try to grow bladders because they are less complex than other organs, such as hearts or livers.

The doctors removed the dogs' own bladders and implanted the lab-grown bladders. One month after transplant, the lab-grown bladders began functioning like the dogs' natural bladders. The scaffolding disintegrated after three months. New blood vessels and nerve endings grew. One surprise was that the dogs gained control over their lab-grown bladders. This eliminated the need for catheters, which are medical instruments used to drain urine from the bladder when the body can't perform this function.

The study lasted nearly one year. The dogs were killed at various intervals throughout the study so the scientists could inspect the lab-grown bladders. In the future, doctors hope that lab-grown bladders can be used to help an estimated 400 million people worldwide who have a diseased or damaged bladder due to cancer, birth defects, nerve damage, or injury.

Atala and his team are trying to grow a kidney in the lab. But kidneys are more complex than bladders. Lab-grown kidneys could save the lives of people who need kidney transplants. In 2002 an estimated 51,000 people were waiting for kidney transplants, but only an estimated 13,372 kidneys were available.

Growing a heart in the laboratory is the ultimate challenge. This organ's structure is extremely complex. It includes an

A researcher displays a strip of cultured (lab-grown) human skin. Technology similar to that used to grow this skin is being developed to grow other, more complex human organs.

intricate network of chambers and blood vessels. But hearts are desperately needed for transplants. Heart disease is the number one killer in the United States—every thirty-three seconds someone dies from it. In response to the organ shortage and xenotransplantation problems, a group of researchers from the United States, Canada, Europe, and Japan formed an organization called Living Implants from Engineering (LIFE). These researchers are trying to grow a human heart in the lab. The project's overall price tag is estimated at billions of dollars. They expect it will take at least another half century before a lab-grown heart will be ready for human transplantation.

A few lab-grown products, such as cartilage and skin, are already being used on humans. Lab-grown skin is being used to treat skin ulcers, which are open sores that do not readily heal and are often a result of poor circulation. The long-term goal is to grow new skin for burn victims. Each year an estimated 150,000 people end up in the hospital with serious burns. Of these burn victims, an estimated 18,000 need skin grafts. The skin graft procedure involves cutting away the dead tissue and then covering the wounds with skin from a cadaver (dead human body) or unburned skin from another part of the patient's body. The supply of cadaver skin available for transplant is limited. Lab-grown skin is a solution to the problem.

STEM CELL CONTROVERSY

Controversy surrounds the process of tissue engineering because it involves the use of stem cells. One source of stem cells is human embryos. The embryos used in stem cell research are usually those left over from in vitro fertilization procedures to help women become pregnant. In vitro fertilization involves removing eggs from a woman's ovary and fertilizing them outside her body to produce embryos that can then be placed in her uterus to develop. The procedure usually results in the production of extra embryos that can be frozen in case the parents would like other children in the future. Parents also have the

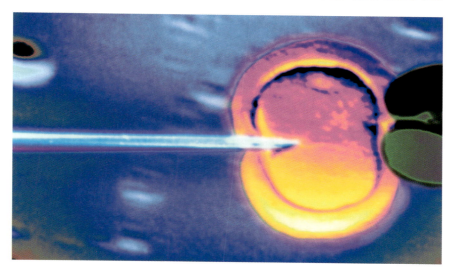

A scientist inserts a needle into a human egg to fertilize it with sperm outside the womb in a process called in vitro fertilization.

option to donate their extra embryos to infertile couples or to stem cell research.

The use of embryonic stem cells in tissue engineering requires destroying a human embryo, which many people consider to be a human life. Others, however, view embryos as simple cellular life because they consist of only a few cells.

As an alternative to embryonic stem cells, adult stem cells have shown promise for treating a variety of diseases. Adult stem cells can be harvested from a patient's own body, eliminating both ethical controversy and immune rejection issues. Unfortunately, adults have only small numbers of stem cells, making them difficult to harvest and purify. Adult stem cells may be more difficult to transform into specialized cells than embryonic stem cells. And a patient's own stem cells may already contain the disease that the doctors are trying to cure.

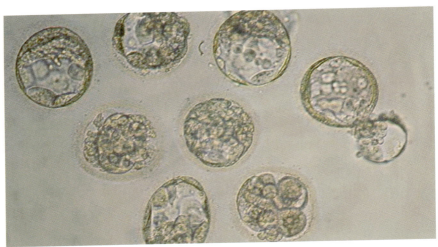

South Korean scientists created these cloned human embryos in 2004 to harvest stem cells for scientific research. Critics argue that it is unethical to clone human embryos for any reason.

Stem cells can also be obtained from cloned human embryos. Scientists at ACT successfully cloned a human embryo by performing the same process used to clone cows, sheep, and monkeys. They extracted the DNA from a human egg cell. Then they inserted the DNA from an adult body cell into it. The cell divided until it was an embryo consisting of six cells. Since the researchers did not place the embryo in a woman's womb, it did not grow into a fully developed baby. "Scientifically, biologically, the entities we are creating are not individuals. They're only cellular life," said Michael West, chief executive officer of ACT.

It is against U.S. law to use government money to perform human cloning research, but ACT did not break any laws. ACT is a private company funded by private investors. Their money can legally be spent on human cloning research. Efforts are under way, however, to pass a law that would make any form of human cloning illegal.

Supporters of stem cell research and human cloning believe that science can use these techniques to fight life-threatening diseases such as heart disease, diabetes, cancer, and AIDS. They hope that in the end, the research will help find cures for many diseases.

Those who are opposed to stem cell research and human cloning are usually also opposed to abortion. They believe that the development of human beings should be in the hands of God, not scientists. They are also concerned that human cloning will go beyond the production of stem cells to become a way of producing fully developed humans.

Some groups have views closer to the middle of the road. They oppose reproductive cloning, or cloning as a means of creating a new, fully developed human being. They do not, however, oppose therapeutic cloning, the cloning of human embryos to produce stem cells.

Chapter 5

PLANT ODDITIES

Farmers are constantly plagued by various problems such as pests, droughts, flooding, and high expenses in their effort to grow food to feed the world. The total population of the world is about 6.2 billion, and it is estimated that 800 million people—almost three times the total population of the United States—are suffering from starvation. In the next twenty-five years, the world population is expected to increase to 7.7 billion. This increase could seriously strain farmers' ability to produce enough crops. To increase crop production, scientists have been working with farmers to solve some of their agricultural problems.

THE FARMER AND BIOTECHNOLOGY

Pests such as the corn rootworm and the Colorado beetle destroy crops. Many farmers use pesticides to control these insects, but the pesticides can also poison nonharmful insects and animals that come into contact with the crops. Pesticides can also harm the environment. Rain washes pesticides into streams, killing fish and other aquatic life and polluting the water that other animals, including humans, drink. Because pesticides are often sprayed onto crops, they become airborne and can travel some distance. Insects and other animals in nearby areas are often exposed.

Opposite: *A Colorado potato beetle feeds on a potato plant. These beetles cause millions of dollars in crop damage each year.*

In response to this problem, scientists at Monsanto Company have genetically modified corn seeds to grow into crops that are resistant to pests. The goal is to eliminate the need for the 8.5 million pounds (3.9 million kg) of insecticides used each year to kill corn crop pests.

KILLER PLANTS

The corn rootworm is the larva stage of a beetle. The larva eats the roots of corn plants. Without roots, corn plants cannot absorb water and nutrients, so they die. The adult beetles eat the stalks and ears of corn.

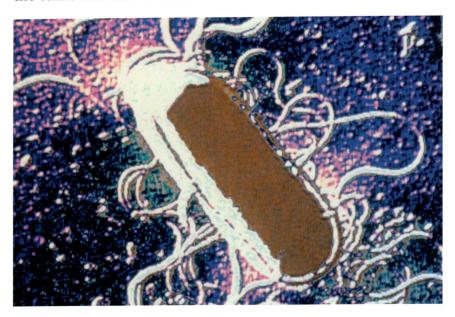

Bacillus thuringiensis (Bt) (above) *is a natural pesticide, lethal to many insects. Scientists have learned how to genetically add Bt's pesticide quality to crops such as corn and potatoes, creating "killer" plants.*

One natural enemy of the corn rootworm is *Bacillus thurin-giensis* (Bt). Bt is a soil bacterium that kills the corn rootworm by poisoning its digestive system. Many organic farmers use the bacterium as a natural pesticide. Bt kills the corn rootworm, but it is not dangerous for humans.

Scientists found the Bt gene *cry9C,* which produces the protein that kills rootworms. Then they added it to the corn DNA. The result was a pesticide-producing plant that is known as "killer corn." Pesticide-producing versions of other crops have also been developed.

Growing cotton involves the use of a lot of pesticides, but the cotton bollworm pest is resistant to many of them. In 1996 Bt cotton seeds became commercially available to farmers, and the results have been promising. Bt cotton has helped control the cotton bollworm, increasing the production of cotton in the United States and decreasing the amount of pesticides sprayed on crops. Farmers in the United States grow an estimated 2,000,000 acres (800,000 ha) of Bt cotton—an area about the size of Hawaii.

Potatoes have also been genetically modified to produce the Bt pesticide. Since 1995 farmers in Idaho have been growing New Leaf potatoes, which kill the Colorado beetle. This pest destroys potato crops by stripping the plants of their leaves.

Not all pesticide-producing genetically engineered plants carry the Bt gene. For example, scientists have created a McIntosh apple that makes its own fungicide to kill *Venturia inaequalis,* a fungus that causes black scabs on apples. The apple was genetically modified to produce a protein called chitinase that occurs naturally in a fungus called *Trichoderma*. When the scab-causing *Venturia inaequalis* fungus comes into contact with chitinase, it is destroyed.

Food crops have also been genetically modified for reasons other than pest control. Scientist Ingo Potrykus spent thirty years creating "golden rice," which gets its yellow color from daffodil flower genes. Potrykus added the genes to the rice genome to enrich the grain with beta carotene, a chemical that the body converts into vitamin A. The goal of this genetically modified creation is to provide vitamin-packed food to starving children in underdeveloped countries. Vitamin A deficiency causes 350,000 children to go blind every year. It also increases children's susceptibility to life-threatening infectious diseases that cause one million deaths each year.

FRANKENFOOD

Farmers who grow genetically modified crops have higher yields and are less reliant on pesticides. Yet heated controversy surrounds the consumption of genetically modified food. Critics call genetically modified food "Frankenfood." They are concerned about the effects genetically modified foods could have on the health of humans and on the environment.

Scientists test genetically modified foods by feeding them to mice in doses much greater than those humans would consume. So far, mice have survived the consumption of genetically modified food without any side effects. Researchers also compare the molecular structure of each genetically modified food with that of the unmodified version of the same food. So the New Leaf potato would be compared molecule by molecule to an unmodified potato. A scientific instrument called a mass spectrometer is also used to test whether genetically modified and unmodified versions of a food are chemically identical. If they are, the food is deemed safe to eat.

Beneficial or monstrous? Genetically modified crops have the potential to feed people worldwide, but many of the long-term health and environmental effects of these crops are unknown.

Despite the results of these tests, some critics are convinced that genetically modified food should not be consumed. Greenpeace, an international group of environmental activists, is one of the organizations that oppose genetically modified food.

"We feel that this is a mass genetic experiment that's going on in our environment and diet," said Charles Margulis of Greenpeace. "Nobody knows what the consequences are going to be, and the untoward [unfavorable] side effects will be irreversible. You can't recall genes once they're released into the environment."

Have You Eaten Genetically Modified Food?

Since 1994, genetically modified foods have been consumed in the United States. Below is a partial list of foods and beverages that contain GM ingredients. To find out more about genetically modified foods, visit www.truefoodnow. org.

7-Up	Hawaiian Punch
Beefaroni	Kellogg's Pop-Tarts
Chef Boyardee	Kool-Aid
Chips Ahoy!	Oreos
Coca Cola	Pepsi Cola
Doritos corn chips	Spaghetti O's
Eggo frozen waffles	Sprite
Gatorade	Teddy Grahams

One of the main concerns of critics is the possible presence of allergens in genetically modified food. A food allergen is a protein in food that causes allergic symptoms such as hives, breathing difficulty, diarrhea, vomiting, loss of consciousness, and even death. Approximately 1 to 2 percent of people in the United States are allergic to one or more foods.

If a particular kind of food particle isn't broken down by stomach acids and enzymes during digestion, the body's immune system may consider it to be harmful. The immune system creates antibodies to fight the allergen. The next time that particular food is consumed, the immune system bombards the body with chemicals in an effort to protect itself. These chemicals cause allergic symptoms.

One of the ways scientists test for allergens in genetically modified food is to replicate the human digestion process and time how long it takes for the food to break down. If the food doesn't break down rapidly enough, it is considered an allergen.

Starlink corn has been genetically modified to contain the *cry9C* gene from Bt, which makes the corn resistant to pests such as the European corn borer and the black cutworm. When the Starlink corn was tested for allergens, scientists noted that it didn't break down quickly enough in the human digestive system. It was considered risky for humans to eat. The same test was used to determine that Starlink corn was suitable for animal consumption. The Environmental Protection Agency (EPA) stipulated that Starlink corn could be fed to animals, but should not be eaten by people.

Greenpeace decided to run some tests on corn products that were randomly picked from a U.S. grocery store. They sent the foods to a lab to be tested for the presence *cry9C*. They wanted to know for sure that the genetically modified corn had not

Japanese consumer activist Keisuke Amagasa displays a bag of cornmeal found to contain Starlink corn in the early 2000s. Critics argue that once genetically modified organisms are out of the lab, there is no way to control them.

gotten into the human food supply. The lab found that Taco Bell brand taco shells contained Starlink corn. This finding was later confirmed by the FDA. The taco shells were immediately recalled from stores.

Starlink corn was also found in foods in Japan, Korea, Denmark, and the United Kingdom. The controversy surrounding Starlink showed that farmers do not always keep genetically modified corn separate from unmodified corn. The American Farm Bureau Federation told seed suppliers that their members were willing to plant only those genetically modified crops that had been approved for both human and animal consumption. Starlink corn is no longer sold.

Genetically modified foods have been consumed in the United States since 1994. Some consumer advocacy groups and other critics believe that any product that contains genetically modified ingredients should be labeled to make it easier to keep track of any adverse reactions to the foods. Food manufacturers who use genetically modified ingredients, however, believe that since the foods have been tested and are considered safe to eat, there is no need to label them as genetically modified.

MUTATIONS AND CONCERNS

Another concern that farmers and environmentalists have about crops that produce their own pesticides is the risk of mutating pests. Some pests survive any application of pesticides. These insects are resistant to the pesticides. When the survivors breed, some of their offspring will be resistant to the pesticides as well. In time, the majority of pests will be resistant, leaving farmers without effective pesticides.

Many organic farmers use Bt to control pests. They fear, however, that overuse of Bt in genetically modified plants will reduce the effectiveness of this useful natural pesticide and they will be left with no way to control damage to their crops.

Monsanto, the company that creates Bt-modified plants, has anticipated this risk. They intend to vary the toxin slightly over time to help reduce resistance. The company also advises farmers to plant unmodified crops near the GM crops. This will make it more likely that pests that survive the digestion of Bt plants will mate with nonresistant pests from the unmodified crop fields. This will keep as much variation as possible in the pests' gene pool so the Bt-resistance gene will have less chance of expressing itself in future generations.

Cause for further concern came to light when a scientific study revealed that Bt toxin is released from the roots of Bt-modified plants. The toxin, which doesn't break down easily, leaches (seeps) into the soil. The poison kills nonharmful insects and other organisms that live in the soil.

THE MONARCH BUTTERFLY

Every year millions of monarch butterflies migrate across the United States. The butterflies lay their eggs on milkweed plants, weeds that often grow in and near cornfields. When the monarch caterpillars hatch from the eggs, their only food is the leaves of milkweed plants.

Scientist John Losey of Cornell University wanted to find out if Bt-producing corn harmed the monarch butterfly. In his laboratory, Losey sprinkled one batch of milkweed leaves with pollen from Bt corn and another with pollen from unmodified corn. (Pollen consists of powdery, yellowish grains containing the male reproductive cells of seed plants.) One group of monarch caterpillars fed on the leaves with Bt corn pollen, and another group fed on the leaves with unmodified corn pollen. The caterpillars that ate the milkweed sprinkled with Bt corn pollen ate less than their non-Bt-eating counterparts. They didn't grow as quickly, and a higher percentage of them died before reaching adulthood than those that ate leaves sprinkled with unmodified corn pollen. This suggests that Bt corn is harmful to the monarch butterfly population.

The results of this experiment outraged the critics of genetically modified food. The damage that the Bt corn might cause to the monarch butterfly strengthened their arguments. Scientists are trying to determine if the laboratory results are the same as results in cornfields. A couple of points need to be examined. One is whether the amount of Bt pollen that caterpillars are likely to eat in the fields is enough to kill them. Another point is whether Bt pollen can actually travel far enough to coat milkweed plants adjacent to cornfields. Since Bt pollen is heavy, the wind may not be able to carry it very far. Examining these points has been tricky. Scientists are still unsure of the extent of the damage, if any, that Bt pollen inflicts on the monarch butterfly.

ACCIDENTAL CROSSBREEDING

Another concern about growing genetically modified plants is the crossbreeding of GM plants with unmodified plants in the wild. Such crossbreeding has occurred in Mexico. Even though growing genetically modified crops is against the law in Mexico, one-fourth of the corn that is imported into that country is genetically modified. The imported GM corn, which is not labeled as such, is supposed to be used for human consumption and for animal feed. It is not intended to be planted. It is believed that the some of the unlabeled Bt corn imported from the United States was unknowingly planted by Mexican farmers.

Scientists discovered the genetically modified plants by accident. They had gone to remote regions of Mexico searching for naturally occurring varieties of corn. When scientists tested the ancient breeds of corn in the laboratory, however, they recognized a genetic marker (an easily identifiable sequence of DNA) that is commonly used in the genetic modification process.

Controversy erupted when it was discovered that genetically modified corn was crossbreeding with natural Mexican varieties.

Corn is sacred in Mexican culture. The native people's ancestors believed the gods created humans from an ear of corn. "It's a worse attack on our culture than if they had torn down the cathedral of Oaxaca and built a McDonald's over it," said Hector Magallone of Greenpeace.

The Mexican Environment Ministry, however, believes that the extent of crossbreeding is minimal. The *Bt* gene is recessive—plants produce Bt toxin only if they received the *Bt* gene from both parent plants—so it probably won't be expressed in future generations of corn.

PLANT PHARMACEUTICALS

Vaccines help prevent humans from catching deadly diseases. Many vaccines, such as those for polio and the measles, are routinely given to children in the United States. However, in poorer, developing countries, many children do not receive the vaccines because they are too expensive or difficult to obtain. As a result, an estimated three million people, mostly children under the age of five, die every year from preventable infectious diseases such as hepatitis B, Hib disease, and yellow fever.

In 1990 scientist Charles Arntzen attended a meeting sponsored by the World Health Organization (WHO). During the meeting, he learned about the Children's Vaccine Initiative, whose goal is to vaccinate children around the world. While Arntzen was visiting Thailand, a developing country, he saw a mother give her baby a banana so the baby would stop crying. Arntzen realized that in poorer countries a banana is a treat, like a cookie is in the United States. The idea of creating bananas that produced vaccines popped into Arntzen's mind.

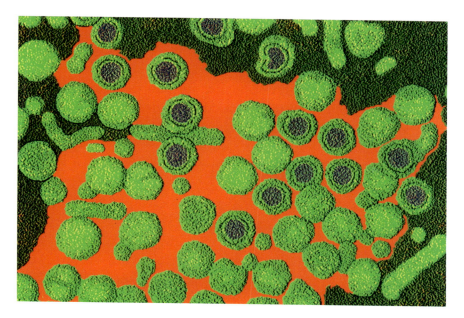

A microscopic photograph of the hepatitis B virus. Scientists are researching ways to genetically modify plants to contain edible vaccines that help fight hepatitis and other diseases.

Edible vaccines offer many advantages. No needles would be needed to administer them. Needles pose a problem because when they are used, they become contaminated with any bacteria or viruses that are present in the patient's bloodstream. If a contaminated needle is reused, it spreads disease rather than controlling it. Edible vaccinations would also be painless and perhaps even tasty. Bananas grow easily in many developing countries, and, unlike bottles filled with medicine, bananas don't require costly refrigeration.

Genetically modifying bananas is more difficult than modifying some other plants. Arntzen began his research by trying to genetically modify a tobacco plant, since it's easier to manipulate than a banana plant.

Different methods of creating a vaccine-producing plant are available. One involves inserting into the plant's cells genes that produce proteins to fight specific human diseases. Another method involves inserting the specified genes into a plant virus, then infecting plants with the virus. The virus then replicates in the plants' cells.

The results of Arntzen's first experiment proved that his theory was correct: plants could be genetically modified to produce vaccines. He then moved on to potato plants, which are more complex than tobacco plants.

The vaccine-producing potato was designed to provide protection from the Norwalk virus. Although it is not deadly in the United States, the Norwalk virus can be fatal to people in poorer countries. The virus causes nausea, vomiting, diarrhea, stomach cramps, headache, and fever. The virus is spread in human feces, so when people don't wash their hands before

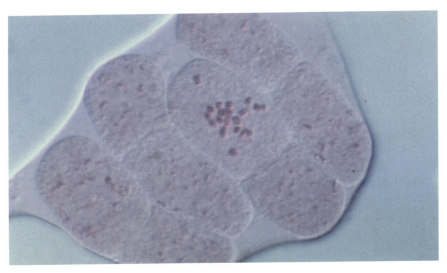

This banana cell contains foreign genetic material (cluster of small dots) introduced by scientists. Genetically modified bananas and other storable fruits and vegetables could provide edible vaccines for humans.

handling food, the food may become contaminated with the virus. Then the people who eat the food may get sick.

Genetically modified potatoes were fed to twenty people over a three-week period. The potatoes had to be eaten raw because the heat of cooking could destroy the vaccine. In the following two months, those who ate the genetically modified potatoes had their blood tested to see if their bodies had produced antibodies to the Norwalk virus. The tests showed that nineteen of the twenty people had increased levels of antibodies in their system.

Vaccines have also been engineered into tomatoes. The drawback with tomatoes is they can't be stored for very long. Other plants that scientists consider good candidates for vaccine production are lettuce, carrots, peanuts, rice, wheat, corn, and soybeans.

Before vaccine-producing food can be distributed, some obstacles must be overcome. Although the plants don't produce large amounts of the vaccine, if a person were to eat too much of the modified food, the vaccine would actually hinder the person's immune response to the infection. Therefore, a way of controlling the dose must be figured out and put into place.

"I don't see a village banana tree with vaccines in it, where everyone goes up and takes one when they want to," said Arntzen. "This is a medicine. I think something like a baby food puree, so you can make tens of thousands of little containers of a banana baby food, and you can sample each one and verify that the dosage is uniform, that they're free of any sort of bacterial toxins or anything else, the standard sort of stuff that has to be done with any pharmaceutical product. . . . [W]e can use food-processing technology, which is available in the developing world, and apply it to medicine."

Another concern is that vaccine-producing plants might crossbreed with unmodified plants, creating a health and environmental problem. The medicine-producing plants would have to be grown separately from plants intended for food. This would help to ensure that the medicine-producing gene would not work its way into the normal food supply through cross-pollination (the transfer of pollen from one flower to another to fertilize the second flower's female reproductive cells). Alternatively, scientists could make the vaccine-producing plants sterile.

Before edible vaccines can be distributed throughout the world, they must meet strict safety guidelines. Clinical trials will have to be conducted. This is an arduous and costly undertaking. But ultimately Arntzen hopes to ship seedlings to underdeveloped countries so people can grow the edible vaccines locally and save millions of lives.

NOVEL PLANT PRODUCTS

Scientists have also genetically modified plants to create novel products for human use. To reduce our dependency on oil for manufacturing plastic, researchers have genetically engineered plants that make plastic. One biotechnology company created cotton plants that produce polyester fibers, a form of plastic. To do this, the researchers used a gene gun that shot gold beads coated with genes into cotton plant seedlings. The genes contained instructions for the production of plastic. The plants produce just a small amount of plastic in the hollow center of their cotton fibers. The goal is to continue to modify the plants so they will produce more plastic. Then the polyester-filled cotton fibers could be used to manufacture shirts that don't need to be ironed and won't fade in the wash.

A researcher sets up a gene gun to introduce transgenic material into a plant cell. A gene gun's high pressure forces gold particles covered with genetically modified material into the nuclei of cells. Gene guns are an alternative to viral vectors.

At the Institute for Plant Genetics and Crop Plant Research in Germany, scientist Udo Conrad inserted the golden orb-weaver spider's silk-producing gene into potato and tobacco plants. The result was plants that produced spider silk, which can be made into a variety of useful products.

Researchers at Michigan Technological University genetically modified aspen trees to produce less lignin. Lignin is a sticky substance that is bleached out of wood during the papermaking process, leaving behind the cellulose fibers that are processed into paper, chemicals, and fuel alcohol. Scientist Vincent Chiang and his team of researchers "knocked out" an aspen tree gene that is involved in producing lignin.

The genetically modified trees produce half as much lignin as unmodified aspens and 15 percent more cellulose. Since the trees don't produce as much lignin, a smaller quantity of chemicals is needed for the paper-manufacturing process. This will make the paper industry more environmentally friendly. Scientists want to duplicate this process on the kinds of trees that are used the most for paper production. But those trees are harder to genetically manipulate than aspens.

Researchers at Washington University in Saint Louis, Missouri, are trying to genetically modify plants to make them smaller. Scientist Michael Neff discovered a mutant gene that controls the growth of plants. The mutant gene is called *BAS1*. Each plant contains hormones that regulate how tall it will grow. The *BAS1* mutant gene tells plant cells to destroy the growth hormones, which in turn stops the growth of the plant.

Neff and his team of researchers were successful in transferring the *BAS1* mutant gene into a tobacco plant that usually grows 6 feet (2 m) tall. The *BAS1* gene stunted the plant's growth to only 6 inches (15 cm).

The scientists want to duplicate the experiment for hedges, grasses, fruit and nut trees, and poplar trees. Smaller hedges could be more attractive in someone's yard. Naturally shorter grass would not have to be mowed. Smaller fruit and nut trees would allow growers to plant more trees per acre and harvest more produce.

TERMINATOR SEEDS TERMINATED

Leading biotech company Monsanto developed crop seeds that grow into plants that produce sterile seeds. Some farmers save seeds from the current crop to plant the next year. But if their crops produced sterile seeds, the farmers would be forced to buy more seeds every year.

Monsanto has invested a great deal of time, research, and money in developing GM crops such as pesticide-producing corn. It is common practice for a company to file a patent when it has invented a new technology. A patent gives the company protection against others that might try to copy their unique technology and make money from it. By developing plants that grew sterile seeds, Monsanto had taken an additional step to protect its investment.

To use Monsanto's seeds, farmers must sign an agreement stating that the seed produced as their crops mature will not be planted the next year. The farmers agree that they will come back to Monsanto and buy more seeds the following year. The problem for Monsanto is that this agreement is difficult to enforce, especially in remote, foreign locations.

Monsanto thought they had solved a dilemma when they decided to sell seeds that produced sterile plants. In a joint effort with the U.S. Department of Agriculture, the Delta and Pine Land Company (a company later acquired by Monsanto) had genetically engineered the seeds. They had inserted a gene that produces a toxin that makes plants sterile. Since the scientists needed to produce enough viable seeds for planting, they also inserted "blocker DNA." The blocker DNA is a set of genetic instructions that suppresses the killer toxin gene until the plant matures. Once the plant matures, the gene that produces the toxin is turned on and causes the plant to become sterile. Seeds that are to be planted are washed in a solution that removes the blocker DNA. Farmers can then plant the seeds to grow crops, but when the plants mature, the seed they produce will be sterile.

When the Rural Advancement Foundation International (RAFI), a farm advocacy organization later renamed ETC Group, learned about the sterile seeds, they organized a protest. The organization used the Internet to inform people of the sterile seeds, which they called "terminator seeds." They also conducted a successful e-mail campaign. Thousands of people from all over the world e-mailed the USDA in protest.

RAFI opposed the sterile seeds because they believed that they gave Monsanto too much control over the seed market. Farmers would be locked into buying the seeds from Monsanto year after year, and Monsanto would be able to charge as much as they wanted for the seeds. The situation would be especially hard on farmers in developing countries, who usually don't have enough money to buy new seeds each year.

Monsanto believed that their genetically modified seeds would produce larger yields than seeds that had not been modified. Since farmers would be able to produce more food, they would make more money, and they would have enough money to buy new seeds the following year.

The activists were also concerned that the modified seeds might cross-pollinate with unmodified plants. Such crossbreeding could potentially wipe out other plants by rendering them sterile. Some activists who were not associated with RAFI were so outraged by this possibility that they burned some test fields where the company was growing the sterile seeds. Monsanto said that the risk of cross-pollination between plants grown from the sterile seeds and plants in the wild was minimal. Some wild plants self-pollinate, and others are receptive to pollination at different times of the year than the genetically modified plants, so they couldn't cross-pollinate. Monsanto also required farmers to plant border crops around the sterile seeds to keep them from spreading.

The protests against the sterile seeds had an impact. Monsanto decided not to sell the controversial seeds to farmers. The company may still use the seeds for research, however.

〔 ECOTERRORISM

A variety of organizations oppose the production of genetically modified organisms. The organizations have different methods of voicing their concerns. Some groups, such as Greenpeace, stage nonviolent demonstrations to attract media publicity. Other groups are more extreme, resorting to violence to make their point. Such protesters are called ecoterrorists.

Oregon State University scientist Steven Strauss and his research team are creating fast-growing trees, disease-resistant trees, and insect-resistant trees. Ecoterrorists refer to the trees as "frankentrees." Some ecoterrorists destroyed nearly one thousand of the trees by chopping them down or spiking them. Spiking involves hammering a metal rod or other hard material into a tree's trunk to make logging dangerous and often impossible. The ecoterrorists wrote an anonymous letter that said, "The test plots of the *Populus* genus trees . . . were independently assessed and found to be a dangerous experiment of unknown genetic consequences."

The scientists state that they are aware that genetically modified plants can pose a risk to the environment, but they make sure that the modified trees do not reproduce with unmodified plants. They do this by destroying the trees themselves before the trees have a chance to flower and spread their pollen.

Michigan State University scientist Catherine Ives has spent years trying to genetically modify food to help alleviate the food supply shortage in developing countries. The budget for her research is $20 million, of which the biotechnology company Monsanto contributed $2,500. That small contribution was enough to spark the ire of the Earth Liberation Front (ELF). The organization set fire to the building where they believed her research was being conducted, destroying a large section of the building.

A spokesperson for ELF, Craig Rosebraugh, said he didn't know which persons in ELF set the fire, but he did voice their reasons for doing so. "[Ives's] program, in my view, was to coerce people in developing nations into believing they should give up sustainable agricultural practices that have been practiced for years and years, throughout many generations, and rely on Monsanto's genetically engineered crops because that's going to end world hunger," said Rosebraugh.

Ives responded to ELF's statement. "I wonder how much time has been spent by people in this organization in developing countries. I see women hiking for miles to bring firewood in because they've cut down everything around them and have no productive soils. I see children who are malnourished. They do not have sustainable agricultural practices in place in many parts of the world. That is what we are trying to help them develop."

The amount of money Monsanto gave to Ives's research program was relatively small. But ELF said, "It's not the money, it's the morals involved."

Ives responded to that statement by saying, "'It's the morals involved.' Interesting. I don't think there's ever any justification for violence, and certainly not for an attack that very easily could have killed a student on a college campus."

Despite ELF's efforts to try to shut down the research at Michigan State University, Ives has her research center in full operation again. Undeterred, ELF continues to target scientists and their genetic modification research. "If you cause them enough economic damage or economic sabotage to their company, hopefully, they will see that it's in their best interest to stop their unjust acts," said Rosebraugh.

Chapter 6

THE OPPOSITION

Many different groups oppose biotechnology research. Each organization uses different tactics in voicing their opposition. And each has critics speaking out against its activities.

THE UNION OF CONCERNED SCIENTISTS

The Union of Concerned Scientists (UCS) is a group of scientists and engineers that was founded at the Massachusetts Institute of Technology (MIT) in 1969. This independent, nonprofit organization has about fifty thousand members. Their goal is to conduct scientific studies to determine if technology is harming people and the environment.

UCS conducted the experiment studying the effects of *Bacillus thuringiensis* bacteria on the monarch butterfly. UCS has an influential voice in the government at the state and federal levels. The results of their monarch butterfly study influenced the Environmental Protection Agency to impose stricter guidelines for farmers who plant Bt-producing seeds.

Although the UCS scientists are well respected, the organization has been criticized for not presenting accurate facts. For example, in the 1980s, the UCS spoke out against the U.S. government's Strategic Defense Initiative, also known as "Star Wars," a proposed space-based defense against Soviet missiles. A physicist for the UCS presented his scientific facts to Congress.

Opposite: *Opponents of genetic modification protest in Greece in 2004.*

Members of the Union of Concerned Scientists speak out against the Strategic Defense Initiative (SDI). The group also has concerns about genetically modified plants and animals.

Years later, their accuracy was questioned. The UCS still maintains that the physicist's facts were correct.

GENEWATCH UK

GeneWatch UK is based in the United Kingdom, where the controversy over genetically modified organisms is much more heated than in the United States. This nonprofit organization was formed in 1998 by a group of scientists.

GeneWatch's goal is to encourage open debate over the pros and cons of genetic engineering. The organization is not completely opposed to genetic engineering, but it wants the public to be informed and to participate in decision making.

An example of their efforts was the acquisition of a confidential Monsanto report that discussed the company's plan "to promote GM products by attempting to determine which experts get on international scientific committees" and thereby "gain influence with key decision makers in government departments." GeneWatch posted the Monsanto report on its website for the public to download.

FOUNDATION ON ECONOMIC TRENDS

The Foundation on Economic Trends is a small nonprofit organization in Washington, D.C. Jeremy Rifkin, its founder, files lawsuits, issues boycotts, and organizes attention-getting demonstrations to spread his views and raise awareness of the risks involved in the genetic engineering of organisms.

In 1999 Rifkin filed a lawsuit against Monsanto. The lawsuit claimed that Monsanto was bringing genetically modified organisms to market without adequately testing their safety for humans and the environment. It accused Monsanto of fixing the price of the seeds. The lawsuit also said that by licensing the use of the seeds instead of simply selling them to farmers, Monsanto would lock farmers into buying more seeds from the company every year.

Rifkin has been successful in bringing together scientists and nonscientists to speak out against biotechnology. "This revolution affects the most intimate aspect of life on earth, our own biology, the biology of our fellow creatures," said Rifkin. "If ever there was a time when we human beings had to take personal responsibility for the future, this is it."

Although Rifkin speaks out against cloning, genetically modified organisms, biological weapons, and companies claiming patents on genetic organisms, he is not entirely opposed to biotechnology. Rifkin is less critical of genetic engineering for pharmaceuticals, preventive medicine, and genetic screening. Rifkin's views are well respected and sought after by the media.

GREENPEACE

Greenpeace, an international nonprofit organization, was founded in 1971. It has 2.9 million members worldwide. Greenpeace was first organized to protest the United States' use of the Amchitka, Alaska, area for nuclear testing. Greenpeace protested by sailing a ship into the bomb test area. Amchitka has since been made into a bird sanctuary.

The organization has also been involved in the "Save the Whales" campaign. Members have protested whaling by chaining themselves to the anchors and harpoons of whaling ships and chaining a whaling ship to a dock. Their protests have influenced key decision makers to ban commercial whaling.

Greenpeace is opposed to genetically modified food. To protest Kellogg Company's use of GM ingredients in breakfast

Greenpeace activists label foods containing genetically modified ingredients in the early 2000s. Greenpeace argues that such products, if used at all, should be clearly labeled to allow consumers an informed choice.

cereals, a Greenpeace member dressed up as Tony the Tiger. This Tony the Tiger costume, however, had a green face. The protester called himself "Frankentony."

Greenpeace members also stopped a ship carrying GM soybeans off the coast of northern Wales. Two protesters chained themselves to the ship's anchor and others went aboard to demand samples of the soybeans. They created a standoff and generated media attention as a result.

The organization's website states that "Greenpeace is a nonviolent organization that is committed to the right to peaceful protest." But Patrick Moore, a cofounder of Greenpeace who is no longer associated with the organization, believes that Greenpeace has "taken a sharp turn to the ultra-left, ushering in a mood of extremism and intolerance." Moore calls this type of protesting "eco-extremism."

Greenpeace works with experts in science, economics, and politics to conduct research. They disseminate the results of their research and make recommendations for change. In order to maintain their independence, they do not accept money from corporations, governments, or political parties. Their goal is "to ensure the ability of the earth to nurture life in all of its diversity."

PETA

People for the Ethical Treatment of Animals (PETA), an international nonprofit organization founded in 1980, has 700 thousand members. The organization supports "animal rights" as opposed to "animal welfare." To members of PETA, the term *animal welfare* refers to a belief that animals have rights as living creatures but that it is acceptable to use them for the benefit of humankind— for food, for medicine, and to further our scientific knowledge.

The term *animal rights*, on the other hand, means that "animals are not ours to use—for food, clothing, entertainment, or experimentation."

PETA members are opposed to eating meat, drinking milk, wearing furs or leather shoes, using wool blankets, exhibiting animals in zoos or circuses, and using any type of animal as a subject in scientific research. PETA's protest methods involve undercover investigations, attention-getting campaigns, and the use of celebrity endorsements to further their ideas and cause.

PETA helped expose mistreatment of animals by Bobby Berosini, a Las Vegas performer who used orangutans in his show. A PETA member using a hidden video camera taped Berosini beating the animals before each performance. PETA filed a lawsuit against Berosini for animal cruelty, and Berosini was banned from performing in Las Vegas and in Branson, Missouri. The organization has also been successful in closing down scientific research labs by videotaping mistreatment of animals.

McDonald's, the Gap, Gillette, and Benetton are a few of the companies against which PETA has voiced its opposition. Targeting larger companies and getting them to change their ways encourages smaller companies to follow suit.

PETA uses celebrities to endorse their cause. For example, their "I'd Rather Go Naked than Wear Fur" campaign featuring celebrity models Christy Turlington and Tyra Banks garnered much media attention.

"We don't mind taking off our clothes or tossing a pie if that's what it takes," said Ingrid Newkirk, president and founder of PETA. "We would rather do that and make idiots of ourselves than be quiet on an issue. And people appreciate it."

Although PETA's animal rights movement is nonviolent, the organization doesn't state that it opposes violence. When an ani-

The world's first cloned primates huddle together in their kennel in 2000. Organizations such as People for the Ethical Treatment of Animals believe that animal testing is unethical, inhumane, and a violation of animal rights.

mal rights organization that called itself "the Justice Department" mailed threatening letters containing razor blades to eighty-seven scientists who were studying primates, PETA spoke out in favor of the activists. "Perhaps the mere idea of receiving a nasty missive will allow animal researchers to empathize with their victims for the first time in their lousy careers," said Newkirk.

ELF

In 1992 the UK-based environmental group Earth First! rejected violence as a way to protest environmental issues. Members who disagreed with this decision formed Earth Liberation Front (ELF).

ELF has no leader and no headquarters. The members, believed to be mostly high school and college students, remain unknown to one another. The group works in secret, and they communicate with the media by letting the spokesperson for the group speak on their behalf.

In 1996 ELF made its first appearance in the United States. Members glued the doors of McDonald's restaurants shut and spray painted buildings. In that same year, ELF blew up a car in the Willamette National Forest in Oregon.

Since 1996, ELF and its sister organization, the Animal Liberation Front (ALF), have committed more than six hundred illegal acts and caused many millions of dollars in damage. ELF has firebombed buildings, burned down housing developments, destroyed GM crops and trees, and caused $12 million in damage by burning a ski resort in Vail, Colorado. "We characterize them as an underground criminal organization that uses economic sabotage," said Steven Berry, a spokesperson for the Federal Bureau of Investigation (FBI).

"The immediate goal is to cause economic damage," said Craig Rosebraugh, the spokesperson for ELF. The group's

ELF claimed responsibility for burning this housing development in San Diego, California, in the early 2000s. ELF has used similar militaristic tactics against the biotech industry, destroying labs and GM test plots.

website states, "The ELF realizes the profit motive caused and reinforced by the capitalist society is destroying all life on this planet. The only way, at this point in time, to stop that continued destruction of life is to by any means necessary take the profit motive out of the killing."

The organization views itself as nonviolent because no one has been killed as a result of its protests. According to its website, ELF members take "all precautions not to harm any animal (human or otherwise)."

Although ELF members have broken the law numerous times, there have been few arrests or convictions. More states are passing laws that impose tough penalties for destroying research crops, however.

"These are hardened criminals," said Scott McInnis, chairman of the U.S. House Subcommittee on Forests and Forest Health. "They are dangerous, they are well-funded, they are savvy, sophisticated and stealthy, and if their violence continues to escalate, it is only a matter of time before their parade of terror results in a lost human life."

* * * *

For thousands of years, humans have used biotechnology to improve their lives—beginning with the discovery that selective breeding created superior livestock. In recent years, scientists have made life-changing discoveries that have pushed the boundaries of both science and ethics, creating living organisms that were once found only in science fiction. While the recent discoveries have improved and even saved the lives of humans, biotechnology research has opened the floodgates of controversy and public outrage. The future consequences of the creation of mutants, clones, and killer corn are yet to be seen.

BIOTECHNOLOGY TIMELINE

8000 B.C.	Humans begin to domesticate and breed animals and grow potatoes.
4000–2000 B.C.	Humans learn to ferment food and make wine. They use lactic acid bacteria to make yogurt and use yeast to make bread and beer.
500 B.C.	The Chinese make the first antibiotic from moldy soybean curds. The antibiotic is used to treat boils and other skin infections.
A.D. 100	The Chinese use powdered chrysanthemums as the first insecticide.
1590	Zacharias Janssen, a Dutch maker of eyeglasses, invents the compound microscope.
1663	Robert Hooke, the English father of microscopy, describes a "cell" after viewing a sample of tree cork under a two-lensed microscope that he invented.
1675	Antoni van Leeuwenhoek, the Dutch father of microscopy, develops a microscope and is the first to see and describe bacteria in a drop of water.
1761	German botanist Joseph Gottlieb Kölreuter studies hybridization, fertilization, and the development of plants.
1796	Edward Jenner, a British physician, begins developing a vaccine for smallpox.
1830s	Swedish chemist Jöns Jakob Berzelius coins the term *protein*.
	Theodor Schwann, a German physiologist, is first to discover an enzyme (a biological molecule that helps chemical reactions take place). He also contributes to the idea that cells make up all living things.
1857	French chemist Louis Pasteur discovers that fermentation is caused by microorganisms.
1859	British naturalist Charles Darwin publishes his work on the theory of evolution and natural selection.
1865	Gregor Mendel, an Austrian monk, conducts experiments with pea plants. He discovers the laws of heredity, laying the foundation for the science of genetics.
1901	The *Bacillus thuringiensis* (Bt) bacterium is discovered by Ishiwata Shigetane, a Japanese bacteriologist.
1905	William Bateson, a British biologist, coins the word *genetics*.
1909	Danish botanist Wilhelm Johannsen coins the word *gene* and theorizes that genes are carried by chromosomes.
1919	Hungarian engineer Karl Ereky coins the term *biotechnology*.
1928	*Bacillus thuringiensis* (Bt) is tested in Germany as a pesticide against the corn borer.
1941	The term *genetic engineering* is introduced by Danish microbiologist A. Jost.

1944 Canadian Oswald Avery and Americans Colin MacLeod and Maclyn McCarty prove that deoxyribonucleic acid (DNA) contains genetic information.

1952 American biologists Robert Briggs and Thomas King produce the first cloned animal: a frog.

1953 James Watson, an American biochemist, and Francis Crick, a British biophysicist, describe DNA as having a double helix structure.

1962 James Watson and Francis Crick win a Nobel Prize for discovering the structure of DNA.

Japanese scientist Osamu Shimomura discovers the green fluorescent protein (GFP) in jellyfish.

1966 American scientist Marshall Nirenberg and his colleagues crack the genetic code sequences for amino acids, which form the basis of living cells.

1968 Marshall Nirenberg wins a Nobel Prize for his research on amino acids.

1973 Modern biotechnology emerges as scientists Stanley Cohen and Herbert Boyer discover recombinant DNA (rDNA) technology, also called gene splicing.

1982 Insulin produced by genetically modified bacteria is approved by the FDA for human use.

1983 Scientists transfer genes to tobacco and petunia plants to make them resistant to the antibiotic kanamycin. These are the first transgenic plants.

1985 Genetically modified plants are tested in the field for the first time.

1990 Bt corn is field tested.

1994 The Flavr Savr tomato, genetically modified to resist rotting, is approved by the FDA for human consumption.

1997 The first mammal cloned from an adult cell is born in Scotland. It is a sheep named Dolly.

1998 American biologist James Thomson successfully grows human embryonic stem cells in the laboratory.

2000 The thale cress plant becomes the first plant to have its complete genome mapped.

Pigs are cloned to provide organs for human transplants.

2001 Advanced Cell Technology scientists create the first cloned human embryos.

2002 The first cloned kitten is born.

2003 The Human Genome Project is completed.

2004 South Korean scientist Woo Suk Hwang and his colleagues are the first to clone human embryos and extract embryonic stem cells.

GLOSSARY

adult stem cell: a stem cell of an adult human being

allele: a specific variation of a gene. Different alleles result in differences in inherited traits such as hair color.

antibodies: molecular proteins that attack and destroy specific microbes that invade the body

***Bacillus thuringiensis* (Bt):** a soil bacterium that kills insects by poisoning their digestive system

base pair: a pair of chemical bases (adenine and thymine or guanine and cytosine) that forms a rung of the DNA ladder

biotechnology: a branch of biology that involves modifying the genetic material of living cells

cell: the basic unit of any living organism that carries on the biochemical processes of life

chromosome: a rodlike structure that contains DNA and is located in the nucleus of most cells. Humans have forty-six chromosomes.

cloning: creating a genetically identical copy of an organism

crossbreeding: the mating of individuals of different, closely related species

cross-pollination: the transfer of pollen from one flower to another to fertilize the second flower's female reproductive cells

deoxyribonucleic acid (DNA): the molecule that contains genetic information and is passed from parent to child during reproduction. The DNA molecule is shaped like a spiral ladder and is found in the nucleus of most cells.

embryo: an animal in the early stages of development, from the time an egg cell is fertilized until it becomes a fetus with recognizable body structures

embryonic stem cell: a stem cell that originates from an embryo

enzyme: a protein molecule that makes chemical reactions occur more quickly or efficiently

ethics: moral principles used to guide decision making

food allergen: a protein in food that causes allergic symptoms such as hives, breathing difficulty, diarrhea, vomiting, loss of consciousness, and even death

gene: a sequence of DNA base pairs located in a particular position on a chromosome that codes for the production of a protein or proteins

gene pool: the collection of genes of all the individuals in an interbreeding population of organisms

genetic disease: a disorder that is caused, at least in part, by one or more genes

genetic engineering: altering genetic material in the laboratory; also called recombinant DNA technology

genetic marker: an easily identifiable sequence of DNA

genetics: a branch of biology that deals with how living things inherit physical and behavioral characteristics and how these inherited characteristics vary from one individual to another

genome: all the genetic material in the chromosomes of an organism

gestation period: the period of time during which a young animal develops in its mother's body

Human Genome Project: the large-scale, international effort to learn the sequence of genes in humans' chromosomes

hyperacute rejection: organ failure occurring in the first few hours following transplantation. The body's immune system recognizes that the organ is foreign tissue and produces antibodies to attack it.

in vitro fertilization: using laboratory techniques to fertilize egg cells and implanting the resulting embryos into a woman's uterus

mutant gene: a gene that has undergone a change in its nucleotide-base sequence

mutation: a random, accidental change in DNA's nucleotide bases. Mutations may be beneficial or harmful, but most have no effect.

nucleotide: one of the building blocks of DNA. A nucleotide consists of a sugar molecule, a phosphate group, and one of the four bases adenine (A), thymine (T), cytosine (C), and guanine (G).

nucleus: the structure containing genetic information located near the center of each plant or animal cell

pharming: the genetic modification of animals to produce drugs or other products for human use

plasmid: a ring of DNA in a bacterial cell

pollen: powdery, yellowish grains containing the male reproductive cells of seed plants

protein: a large molecule made according to instructions from a gene. Proteins are the building blocks of life, making up cells, organs, and tissues.

recombinant DNA technology: another name for genetic engineering

reproductive cloning: cloning as a means of creating human or animal life

resistance: the ability of an organism to remain unaffected by a disease or poison

selective breeding: the breeding of plants and animals to produce specific desirable traits

stem cell: a generalized cell that has the ability to transform into any kind of specialized cell, such as a brain cell or a blood cell

sterile: unable to reproduce

surrogate: a human woman or female animal into which an embryo is implanted to continue its development

telomere: the tip of a chromosome. Each time a cell divides, the telomeres become shorter. Because telomeres do not contain genes, no vital genetic information is lost during cell division.

therapeutic cloning: the cloning of human embryos to produce stem cells

tissue engineering: the process of growing tissue from stem cells in the laboratory

toxin: a poison

transgenic organism: an organism that contains one or more genes from another species

vaccine: a substance containing killed, disabled, or live organisms that is given orally or by injection to produce or increase immunity to a particular disease by causing the body to produce antibodies to the organism

vector: a means of moving genes from one organism to another. Most vectors used in genetic engineering are made from disabled viruses.

virus: the simplest kind of life-form, consisting of a protein shell surrounding a core of DNA. Viruses are so tiny that they can be seen only through the most powerful microscopes.

xenotransplantation: the process of transplanting organs from one species to another

zygote: a fertilized egg cell

SOURCE NOTES

Introduction

6–7 Steve Sternberg, "Monkey Glows Green, for Human Benefit," *USA Today,* January 12, 2001, 1A.

7 James Meek, "ANDi, First GM Primate: Will Humans Be Next?" *Guardian,* January 12, 2001.

7 Amanda Onion, "Man-made Monkey." ABC News, January 12, 2001, http://www.abcnews. com (May 2002).

Chapter 1

15 "The Biotech Industry," *The North Carolina Biotechnology Center,* May 10, 2002, http://www.ncbiotech.org/ careers/bioindy.cfm (May 2002).

Chapter 2

22 Maya Pines, "Why So Many Errors in Our DNA?" *Blazing a Genetic Trail,* n.d., http://www.bioeducation.org/ genetictrail/errors/wyso.htm (May 2002).

Chapter 3

33 Ian Austen, "Silk and Money," *Canadian Business,*" June 26, 2000, 42–45.

34 Ibid.

38 "Disease Resistant Bull Cloned at Texas A&M," *Texas A&M Agricultural News Page,* December 18, 2000, http://www.cvm.tamu. edu/news/bull86 (May 2002).

40 Kris Axtman, "Quietly, Animal Cloning Speeds Onward," *The Christian Science Monitor,* October 15, 2001, http://www. csmonitor.com/2001/1015/ p3s1-ussc.html (December 2004).

42 "Africa Malaria Day Facts and Figures," *World Health Organization,* 2002, http://mosquito.who.int/amd/ abuja2002_facts.htm (December 2004).

51 Gareth Cook, "Cross Hare: Hop and Glow," *Boston Globe,* September 17, 2000, A01.

Chapter 4

54–55 "Organ Farm," *Frontline,* prod. Ben Loeterman and Frank Simmonds, dir. Frank Simmonds, PBS, March 27, 2001.

56 Ibid.

56 Vida Foubister, "Ethics of Xenotransplantation Considered," *American Medical News,* December 11, 2000, 17.

56 "Organ Donation and Transplantation," *United Network for Organ Sharing,* May 2002, http://www. unos.org (December 2004).

61 "Lab-Grown Bladder Encourages Scientists," *CNN,* January 30, 1999, http://www.cnn.com/ HEALTH/9901/30/bladder/ index.html.

61 "Organ Donation and Transplantation" (December 2004).

62 American Heart Association, "Cardiovascular Diseases." *2002 Heart and Stroke Statistical Update,* http://www.americanheart.org/presenter.jhtml?identifier+1200026 (May 2002).

62 Geoffrey Cowley, "Replacement Parts: Medicine," *Newsweek,* January 27, 1997, 66.

65 Michael West, interview by Tim Russert, *Meet the Press,* NBC, November 25, 2001.

Chapter 5

67 "The Issue—Facts and Figures," The Population Institute, http://population.newc.com/teampublish/71_234_1054.CFM (December 2004).

67 "United States Census 2000," *The U.S. Census Bureau Home Page,* http://www.census.gov (December 2004).

68 Marc Kaufman, "A Biotech Boon? Corn Designed to Kill Common Pest Stirs Hope as Pesticide," *Washington Post,* August 18, 2001, A01.

69 Tara Weaver-Missick, "Protecting Farmers' Investment in Bt Cotton," *Agricultural Research,* February 2001, 20–22.

70 J. Madeleine Nash, "Grains of Hope," *Time,* July 31, 2000, 31–38.

71 "Harvest of Fear." *A Frontline/Nova Special Presentation,* writ., prod., and dir. Jon Palfremen, PBS, April 23, 2001.

78 "Mexicans Angered by Spread of GM Corn," CNN News, December 31, 2001, http://www.cnn.com/2001/HEALTH/diet.fitness/12/31/modified.corn.ap/index.html (May 2002).

78 Global Alliance for Vaccines and Immunization (GAVI), *GAVI: The Vaccine Alliance,* http://www.vaccinealliance.org (December 2004).

81 "Harvest of Fear."

87 "Frankentrees?" *American Forests,* Summer 2001, 14.

88 "Harvest of Fear."

88 Ibid.

88 Ibid.

88 Ibid.

89 Ibid.

Chapter 6

92–93 Sturminster Newton, "Monsanto Plays Dirty—Again," *The Ecologist,* November 2000, 11.

93 "Harvest of Fear."

95 John Elvin, "Greenpeace Cofounder Says Eco-Extremists Are Antihuman," *Insight on the News,* September 24, 2001, 34.

95 Greenpeace, http://www.greenpeace.org (December 2004).

96 "About PETA," *PETA: The Animal Rights Organization,* http://www.peta.org (December 2004).

96 Aimee Welch, "Fur Flies in PETA's Fight for Animals," *Insight on the News,* July 17, 2000, 15–17.

97 Ibid.

98 Brad Knickerbocker, "Eco-Terrorists, Too, May Soon Be on the Run," *Christian Science Monitor,* February 15, 2002, 2.

98 Laurent Belsie, "Eco-Vandals Put a Match to 'Progress,'" *Christian Science Monitor,* July 5, 2001, 11.

98 Brandon Bosworth, "America's Homegrown Terrorists," *The American Enterprise,* April/May 2002, 48–49.

99 "FBI Expert Cites Top U.S. Terrorist Group," *San Diego Union-Tribune,* February 12, 2002, A-10.

SELECTED BIBLIOGRAPHY

Campbell, Neil A. *Biology: Concepts & Connections.* 4th ed. San Francisco: Benjamin Cummings, 2003.

Drlica, Karl. *Understanding DNA and Gene Cloning: A Guide for the Curious.* Hoboken, NJ: Wiley, 2004.

Judson, Karen. *Genetic Engineering: Debating the Benefits and Concerns.* Berkeley Heights, NJ: Enslow, 2001.

Watson, James D., et al. *Molecular Biology of the Gene.* 5th ed. San Francisco: Pearson/Benjamin Cummings, 2003.

FURTHER READING AND WEBSITES

BOOKS

Cefrey, Holly. *Cloning and Genetic Engineering.* New York: Children's Press, 2002.

Cohen, Daniel. *Cloning.* Brookfield, CT: Twenty-First Century Books, 2002.

Fridell, Ron. *Decoding Life: Unraveling the Mysteries of the Human Genome.* Minneapolis: Lerner Publications Company, 2004.

Gerdes, Louise I., ed. *Genetic Engineering: Opposing Viewpoints.* Farmington Hills, MI: Greenhaven Press, 2004.

Goodnough, David. *The Debate over Human Cloning.* Berkeley Heights, NJ: Enslow, 2003.

Judson, Karen. *Genetic Engineering: Debating the Benefits and Concerns*. Berkeley Heights, NJ: Enslow, 2001.

Kowalski, Kathiann M. *The Debate over Genetically Engineered Food: Healthy or Harmful?* Berkeley Heights, NJ: Enslow Publishers, 2002.

Lambrecht, Bill. *Dinner at the New Gene Café*. New York: St. Martin's Press, 2001.

Marshall, Elizabeth L. *High-Tech Harvest: A Look at Genetically Engineered Foods*. New York: Franklin Watts, 1999.

Nardo, Don. *Cloning*. San Diego: Lucent Books, 2002.

Walker, Mark, and David McKay. *Unravelling Genes: A Layperson's Guide to Genetic Engineering*. St. Leonards, New South Wales, Australia: Allen and Unwin, 2000.

WEBSITES

About Biotech
http://www.accessexcellence.org/RC/AB
> This National Health Museum webpage contains a wide variety of links covering biotech issues and ethics, applications of biotechnology, and the history of biotech.

DNA from the Beginning
http://www.dnaftb.org/dnaftb
> This site presents the history of genetics and simple explanations of basic concepts.

Foundation on Economic Trends
http://www.foet.org
> This nonprofit organization examines emerging trends in science and technology and their impacts on the environment, the economy, culture, and society.

Frontline: Organ Farm
http://www.pbs.org/wgbh/pages/frontline/shows/organfarm
> This site contains detailed information on xenotransplantation.

Genetic News and Links
http://www.bio.davidson.edu/people/kabales/geneticslinks.html
> Check out this collection of news articles on the genomic revolution, along with links to sites that discuss the history of genetics, the Human Genome Project, cloning, and related topics.

Genetic Science Learning Center
http://gslc.genetics.utah.edu/
> How does genetics affect our lives? Check out the online activities, labs, experiments, and workshops for students who are curious about genetics.

Genewatch UK
http://www.genewatch.org
  GeneWatch UK is a not-for-profit group that monitors developments in genetic technologies, from GM crops and foods to genetic testing of humans.

Greenpeace International
http://www.greenpeace.org
  Greenpeace is a nonprofit group that works to protect the environment.

Human Genome Project Information
http://www.ornl.gov/hgmis/project/about.html
  This U.S. government site houses information the Human Genome Project.

Hypermedia Glossary of Genetic Terms
http://www.weihenstephan.de/~schlind/genglos.html
  This compact site offers basic definitions for and details about genetic terms.

NOVA: 18 Ways to Make a Baby
http://www.pbs.org/wgbh/nova/baby/
  A look at fertility, cloning, and how cells divide.

People for the Ethical Treatment of Animals (PETA)
http://www.peta.org
  PETA is the world's largest animal rights organization.

PBS: Harvest of Fear
<http://www.pbs.org/wgbh/harvest>
  This site has interviews, discussions, video, and more on the topic of genetically modified food. You can virtually modify your own plants.

PBS-Scientific American Frontiers: The Bionic Body: The Body Shop
http://www.pbs.org/saf/1107/features/body.htm
  This site discusses tissue engineering and lab-grown body parts.

Union of Concerned Scientists (UCS)
http://www.ucsusa.org
  UCS is a nonprofit group whose stated goal is to use scientific analysis and citizen advocacy to build a cleaner, healthier environment and a safer world.

Your Genes Your Choices
http://ehrweb.aaas.org/ehr/books/
  Describes basic genetics, as well as the implications of genetic research.

Your Genes, Your Health
http://www.yourgenesyourhealth.org
  This multimedia site gives quick, easy-to-understand details about genetic disorders and their treatments.

INDEX

ABOUT THE AUTHORS

Samantha Seiple holds a master's degree in library and information science, with a concentration in youth services. She has worked as a reference librarian at the San Diego Public Library and as a production editor of science books at Academic Press. She currently resides in San Diego, California, where she is a freelance writer.

Todd Seiple has undergraduate and master's degrees in chemistry and an MBA in finance and marketing. He has worked as a research chemist, making nonradioactive DNA probes for the detection of human diseases and creating pharmaceuticals to aid in the fight against cancer. He is currently an executive at a software company in San Diego.

PHOTO ACKNOWLEDGMENTS

The images in this book are used with permission of: courtesy of National Human Genome Research Institute, p. 6; © PhotoDisc Royalty Free by Getty Images, p. 8; © Charles and Josette Lenars/CORBIS, p. 11; © Jim Zuckerman/CORBIS, pp. 13, 16; courtesy of the USDA APHIS, p. 14; © Getty Images, pp. 19, 22, 47, 64; Bill Hauser, pp. 21, 25, 26, 29; King's College London, p. 24; © Roger Ressmeyer/CORBIS, p. 27; Advanced Cell Technology, Inc., Worcester, MA, p. 28; © Vo Trung Dung/CORBIS SYGMA, pp. 30, 80, 83; © Dr. Dennis Kunkel/Visuals Unlimited, p. 32; © Sean O'Neill/NEXIA Biotechnologies, p. 34; © University of Guelph, Ontario, Canada, p. 37; U.S. Department of Energy Human Genome Program, , <http://www.ornl.gov.hgmis>, p. 40; © Science VU/Visuals Unlimited, p. 43; © Dr. Linda Stannard, UCT/Science Photo Library, pp. 44, 79; © Reuters/CORBIS, pp. 49, 74; © James King-Holmes/Science Photo Library, p. 50; © Victor De Schwanberg/Science Photo Library, p. 52; © Vo Trung (NPP) Dung/CORBIS SYGMA, p. 55; © Dr. Klaus Boller/Science Photo Library, p. 57; © Mauro Fermariello/Photo Researchers, Inc., p. 62; © Lester Lefkowitz/CORBIS, p. 63; © William Weber/Visuals Unlimited, p. 66; © Alfred Pasieka/Science Photo Library, p. 68; © AFP/Getty Images, pp. 71 (left), 90, 92, 94; © Time Life Pictures/Getty Images, p. 71 (right); © OSHU/CORBIS SYGMA, p. 97; © Fred Greaves/Reuters/CORBIS, p. 98.

Cover: © Steve Crise/CORBIS.

OCT   2005